The Pers[ian Gulf] in the Coming Decade

Trends, Threats, and Opportunities

Daniel L. Byman • *John R. Wise*

Prepared for the

United States Air Force

Approved for Public Release; Distribution Unlimited

RAND

Project AIR FORCE

The research reported here was sponsored by the United States Air Force under Contract F49642-01-C-0003. Further information may be obtained from the Strategic Planning Division, Directorate of Plans, Hq USAF.

Library of Congress Cataloging-in-Publication Data

Byman, Daniel, 1967–
    The Persian Gulf in the coming decade : trends, threats, and opportunities /
Daniel L. Byman, John R. Wise.
        p. cm.
    "MR-1528."
    Includes bibliographical references (p.).
    ISBN 0-8330-3206-2
        1. Persian Gulf Region. 2. Persian Gulf Region—Relations—United States.
    3. United States—Relations—Persian Gulf Region. I. Wise, John R. II. Title.

DS326 .B96 2002
953.6—dc21

                                                                    2002026577

RAND is a nonprofit institution that helps improve policy and decisionmaking through research and analysis. RAND® is a registered trademark. RAND's publications do not necessarily reflect the opinions or policies of its research sponsors.

Cover design by Stephen Bloodsworth

© Copyright 2002 RAND

Published 2002 by RAND
1700 Main Street, P.O. Box 2138, Santa Monica, CA 90407-2138
1200 South Hayes Street, Arlington, VA 22202-5050
201 North Craig Street, Suite 202, Pittsburgh, PA 15213-1516
RAND URL: http://www.rand.org/
To order RAND documents or to obtain additional information,
contact Distribution Services: Telephone: (310) 451-7002;
Fax: (310) 451-6915; Email: order@rand.org

PREFACE

This report examines likely challenges to U.S. interests in the Persian Gulf region in the coming decade. In particular, the report explores the conventional military strength of Iran and Iraq, the potential for subversion, and the social and economic weaknesses of all the regional states. In addition, it seeks to identify key uncertainties and trends that may shape the region's future. It then assesses the implications of these trends for the United States, particularly the U.S. military.

The research was completed before the September 11, 2001 terrorist attacks on the United States. These attacks had profound implications not only for America but also for the countries of the Persian Gulf. This report does not address the ramifications of these attacks and the U.S. response; the U.S. campaign is still unfolding and the issues are the subject of current RAND research.

The project was sponsored by the Director of Operational Plans Office of the Deputy Chief of Staff for Air and Space Operations (HQ USAF/XOX) and took place in the Strategy and Doctrine Program of RAND's Project AIR FORCE. Comments are welcomed and may be addressed to the Program Director, Dr. Ted Harshberger.

PROJECT AIR FORCE

Project AIR FORCE, a division of RAND, is the Air Force federally funded research and development center (FFRDC) for studies and analysis. It provides the Air Force with independent analysis of policy alternatives affecting the development, employment, combat

iii

readiness, and support of current and future aerospace forces. Research is performed in four programs: Aerospace Force Development; Manpower, Personnel, and Training; Resource Management; and Strategy and Doctrine.

CONTENTS

FIGURES

TABLES

SUMMARY

The war and instability that have long characterized the Persian Gulf have diminished in the last decade—a shift that calls for a reevaluation of U.S. policy. The conventional military threat to U.S. partners has lessened. However, the Gulf regimes, while generally stable, may face increased popular pressure to curtail ties to the United States, particularly to the U.S. military.

THE DANGER IN THE PAST

The United States and its partners in the Gulf region have faced a range of challenges over the last 25 years. Iraq invaded Kuwait in 1990 and, after being expelled by a massive coalition military effort, has continued to threaten the security of U.S. partners in the region. In 1971, Iran occupied several islands claimed by the United Arab Emirates (UAE). It has since increased its military presence on the islands and has even deployed chemical weapons there during crises. Iran and Iraq's rivalry with each other has at times spilled outside their borders, leading them to bully or subvert U.S. regional partners.

Internal instabilities have also posed a threat to U.S. partners. Iran and Iraq both sponsored terrorism in the Gulf, with Tehran in particular engaged in a range of efforts to overthrow the conservative Gulf monarchies. Islamists in Saudi Arabia have used violence against the regime and U.S. forces. Bahrain suffered widespread communal rioting and unrest in the mid-1990s, as Bahraini Shi'a protested against discrimination and demanded a greater voice in decisionmaking.[1]

THE SHIFTING MILITARY BALANCE

The military balance in the Gulf is far more favorable to the United States and its partners than it was in the past. Iraq's military is weaker in both absolute and relative terms than it was in 1990. Iraqi forces have never recovered from the battering they took from the U.S.-led coalition in Operation Desert Storm. Sanctions have prevented Iraq from importing significant numbers of weapons or upgrading existing systems. Iraqi morale is low, and the officer ranks are heavily politicized.

As a result, it is questionable whether Iraq can initiate, let alone sustain, conventional operations involving more than a few divisions. However, given the proximity of Kuwait to Iraq, the small size of Kuwaiti forces, and the favorable terrain, Iraq could overrun Kuwait if U.S. forces were not present. Baghdad could also deploy several divisions against Jordan, Syria, Iran, and Turkey.

Iraq's ability to rebuild its conventional military forces and revitalize its economy depends heavily on whether sanctions are lifted and what, if any, restrictions remain on the regime. Iraq's weapons of mass destruction (WMD) expertise and programs are considerable and, if sanctions were lifted, the country could gain a nuclear capacity within several years. Another priority for Iraq is to rebuild its chemical, biological, and missile systems.

Iran poses even less of a conventional military threat to the Gulf states than does Iraq. Although Tehran has faced fewer restrictions on its military purchases than has Baghdad in the last decade, its initial military position was far weaker. Iran has not fully recovered

---

[1]The September 11, 2001 terrorist attacks had a profound impact on the Gulf region and on U.S. relations with the Middle East more broadly. The attacks strongly affect U.S. relations with Saudi Arabia and other states whose citizens have provided financial support for and manpower to radical causes. In addition, the U.S. response has considerable implications for the stability of friendly regimes. Nevertheless, this report does not address these issues; the ramifications from the attack and from the subsequent U.S. campaign against terrorism are still unfolding and are the subject of current RAND research.

from the Iran-Iraq war, which killed hundreds of thousands of Iranians and destroyed much of Iran's military equipment. The war also created widespread opposition to military adventurism in general among the Iranian people. Iran's military lacks a dependable supplier, and its budget has been limited in the last decade, although increases in oil prices in the past two years have provided more currency for arms purchases. In addition, Tehran would need far greater capabilities to pose a conventional military threat to the Gulf states because of geography: Iranian forces must conduct amphibious operations across the Persian Gulf or go through Iraqi territory, either of which would be difficult and exponentially more challenging than an Iraqi invasion of Kuwait.

In addition to decreased danger of outright invasion, the threat of Iranian-backed subversion has also fallen in the last decade. Since the mid-1990s, Iran has become far less active in promoting unrest in the Gulf. Tehran has cultivated the goodwill of the Gulf states to improve cooperation in oil pricing and, in general, pursues a less aggressive regional foreign policy. Perhaps most important, the attraction of the Iranian revolution has declined in the Gulf, reducing the number of potential supporters.

Iran still poses a range of potential threats to U.S. interests. Iran could use its clandestine network to subvert an already unstable Gulf state. It could use its limited forces to temporarily deny commercial shipping access to the Gulf. Finally, Iran could seize an island in the Gulf claimed by a U.S. ally or an offshore oil platform. Iran, like Iraq, has pursued a range of WMD programs and it might develop a nuclear weapon in the coming decade.

In addition to the weakness of likely adversaries, the United States has dramatically increased its regional military presence and overall capacity to respond to contingencies. On average, the United States deploys 25,000 personnel in the Gulf region. In addition to the forces it has in the theater, the United States has augmented its cooperation with the Gulf states and its ability to respond rapidly.

MARGINALLY STRONGER GULF PARTNERS

The military balance is increasingly favorable for the United States not only because of the weakness of Iran and Iraq, but also because of the increased relative strength of its Gulf partners. Given the size of their militaries, the amount of advanced equipment the Gulf states have purchased since the Gulf War is staggering; it includes purchases of state-of-the-art fighter aircraft, tanks, armored personnel carriers, and other costly items. The Gulf states have also benefited from closer cooperation with the U.S. military.

Despite the impressive capabilities of their military systems, the Gulf partners would remain dependent on the United States in many contingencies, particularly those involving an Iraqi invasion of Kuwait or Saudi Arabia. The Gulf states' military forces' skills do not match the capabilities of their sophisticated systems. Many of the Gulf states face severe manpower shortages arising from the small base of eligible recruits. Often the Gulf states do not have the necessary support infrastructure for the systems they own. Training and maintenance may be neglected or perfunctory. Regional land forces' capabilities for maneuver warfare are poor, and they lack effective combined arms and joint capabilities. Although several of the Gulf states' air forces are reasonably skilled at air-to-air operations, they have few air-to-ground capabilities.

THE FRAYING SOCIAL CONTRACT

Although the external threats to U.S. interests are limited, the picture is darker when the internal situation of U.S. partners is examined. U.S. partners are not on the brink of revolution or dramatic regime change, but it is likely that economic and social pressures will grow in the coming decade, making it more difficult for these states to cooperate openly and wholeheartedly with the United States.

A number of economic and social problems are undermining the political arrangement that has governed social relations in the Gulf since the discovery of oil. The Gulf states have failed to diversify their economies beyond oil. As a result, in Saudi Arabia, Bahrain, and Oman unemployment is growing and the government is less able to provide the services that many Gulf citizens take for granted. Burgeoning populations, poor education systems, and fluctuations in the price of oil only exacerbate the economic problems.

Governments in the Gulf are under pressure to be responsive, and the potential for unrest is growing. Gulf governments, however, have not established effective political institutions for managing any increased tension. Although these economic, social, and political problems have not caused massive unrest and are not likely to do so, they raise the prospect of greater criticism, limited unrest, and increased tension.

KEY UNCERTAINTIES

Several hard-to-predict factors will shape the Gulf in the coming decade. Iran and Iraq face the potential for massive and chronic instability. A collapse of either regime, or even increased turmoil, could lead to civil strife, refugee flows, and other forms of instability. In addition, neighboring powers might meddle, and Iranian or Iraqi leaders might try to divert domestic attention by becoming aggressive abroad.

The quality of the conventional weapons that Iran and Iraq will possess will in large part be determined by Russia—a major supplier to Iran—and Europe, which currently does not sell major systems to either country. Whether Iran or Iraq will possess advanced surface-to-air missiles and antiship cruise missiles, is trained to use various sophisticated systems, and otherwise is able to acquire the capabilities needed to challenge the United States will depend more on decisions in Moscow or Paris than those in Baghdad or Tehran. During the 1990s, the United States effectively limited the flow of advanced weapons to Iran and to Iraq, but changes in U.S.-Europe or U.S.-Russia relationships could lead to greater problems in the Gulf. The cooperation of outside powers is particularly important to halt Iran and Iraq's WMD programs.

The price of oil is a key question, but the security dynamics of the oil market are often contradictory. On the one hand, a higher oil price will enable Iran and Iraq to purchase more weapons and otherwise sustain their regimes in the face of domestic unrest. On the other hand, a low oil price will hurt U.S. partners as well as adversaries, increasing the risk of political instability in the region.

PREPARING FOR ANTI-U.S. PRESSURE

The U.S. military presence and overall U.S. policy at times increase domestic criticism of the Gulf regimes. Much of the public in the Gulf believes their governments spend heavily on supporting U.S. forces, money that they believe would otherwise be used to alleviate economic hardship. The large U.S. military presence also highlights the failure of area regimes to protect their citizens. Depending on foreigners to provide security is particularly problematic because Western political and religious values are often seen as incompatible with Islamic teachings. This dilemma poses particular problems in Saudi Arabia, whose religious establishment believes that Western values are corrupting and should be kept out of the country. Criticism of U.S. support for Israel is widespread, and many area residents also believe that the United States seeks to perpetuate the suffering of the Iraqi people.

The United States currently has achieved a balance between its military requirements in the Gulf and the ability of regional partners to host and work with U.S. forces. Nevertheless, if domestic unrest increases, the Gulf states may face increased pressure to decrease ties to the United States, particularly those with the U.S. military. Such problems may make the operating environment difficult for the United States. Possible problems include placing limits on U.S. operations, responding slowly during a crisis, limiting support for various U.S. political initiatives in the region, cutting military purchases, and reducing the size or visibility of the U.S. military presence.

ACKNOWLEDGMENTS

Many people gave generously of their time and expertise, greatly strengthening the conclusions in this report. Lt Colonel Michael Davis, General Hugh Cameron (USAF, ret.), David Oemig, and William King offered many insights into the complexities of the region and the resulting complications for U.S. military operations. Geoffrey Kemp and Andrew Parasiliti provided thorough and thoughtful reviews of this document. At RAND, Nora Bensahel, Jerrold Green, Ted Harshberger, C. R. Neu, Jeremy Shapiro, and Alan Vick offered many helpful suggestions and kindly served as a sounding board for a range of ideas and arguments. Risha Henneman's administrative assistance was invaluable, as was that of Leslie Thornton.

Chapter One

INTRODUCTION

War, revolution, unrest, and extremism have plagued the Persian Gulf over the last 25 years. The Iranian revolution, the Iran-Iraq war, a Shi'a Muslim coup attempt in Bahrain, riots and demonstrations in Saudi Arabia, the U.S.-Iran naval clashes during the 1987–1988 reflagging effort, the Iraqi invasion of Kuwait, and the post–Gulf War aggressive containment of Iraq and Iran are only the most visible troubles. Understandably, U.S. policy has focused on defending its partners in the region from the twin threats of military aggression and foreign-backed subversion.[1]

This report argues that strife and radicalism have obscured recent trends toward regional stability—a shift that calls for a reevaluation of U.S. policy. The Gulf states of Kuwait, Saudi Arabia, Oman, Bahrain, Qatar, and the United Arab Emirates (UAE) are more secure now than at any time since the fall of the Shah of Iran. Saddam Husayn's Iraq, while still aggressive, is for the moment defanged in a conventional military sense. Reformers who are more pro-Western and less bellicose in general are gaining power in Tehran. Iran and Iraq's conventional forces are weak as a result of import restrictions, maintenance problems, growing obsolescence, poor training, and

---

[1]Although the September 11, 2001 terrorist attacks had a profound impact on the Gulf region and on U.S. relations with the Middle East more broadly, the implications are not addressed in this report. Clearly, the attacks strongly affect U.S. relations with Saudi Arabia and other states whose citizens have provided financial support for and manpower to radical causes. In addition, the U.S. response has considerable implications for the stability of friendly regimes. Nevertheless, this report does not address these issues; the ramifications from the attack and from the subsequent U.S. campaign against terrorism are still unfolding and are the subject of current RAND research.

limited budgets. Even without the formidable U.S. presence in the region, the two countries pose little danger to their neighbors. The ideological threat also is diminished. The Gulf states have weathered Iranian-inspired and home-grown Islamist unrest, to the surprise of many observers.

Indeed, it is U.S. adversaries, not U.S. partners, that are under siege. The least stable governments in the region today are the noxious regime of Saddam Husayn and the hard-line clerical cabal in Tehran. Although Saddam retains a firm grip on power, he does not exercise control over all of Iraq, let alone his neighbors. Unrest at home continues to simmer, as does ethnic and sectarian tension. Iran's "government of God" is also under siege, albeit a largely quiet one. Since the election of Mohammed Khatami in 1997, Iran's government has slowly shifted its policies from confrontation to conciliation. Yet stability may remain elusive. Even though oil prices rose considerably at the end of the decade and in 2001, Iran's economy has stagnated, and politicians in Tehran may choose a bellicose foreign policy to divert domestic attention from the regime's failures.

Many challenges to U.S. interests in the Gulf remain acute, but they are of a different nature from the ones facing U.S. planners a decade ago. Both Iran and Iraq are pursuing weapons of mass destruction (WMD), and either could acquire conventional systems that would make U.S. military operations more difficult. Gulf regimes, while generally stable, may face increased popular pressure to curtail ties to the United States, particularly those with the U.S. military. Ignoring these changes may lead the United States to prepare for the wrong threat or inadvertently destabilize the very partners it seeks to protect.

U.S. INTERESTS IN THE GULF REGION

The Persian Gulf is a critical region for the United States for a number of reasons.[2] The most important U.S. interest is ensuring the free

---

[2]After the September 11, 2001 attacks, the suppression of terrorism has become the primary U.S. concern in the region. The United States has a strong interest in ensuring that Iran and Iraq do not sponsor terrorism against it or its U.S. allies. In addition, the United States seeks to ensure that nationals in Saudi Arabia or other states in the region do not join terrorist groups or provide them with financial or other assistance.

flow of oil from the region to world markets. States in the Gulf will remain leading oil exporters in the next decade, although the degree of their dominance will depend heavily on the price of oil. Saudi Arabia alone has more than a quarter of the world's total proven reserves; Iraq has the second largest reserves, possessing over 10 percent of the world's total; while Iran, the UAE, and Kuwait have about 9 percent each.[3] By the end of the decade, Iraq's sustainable production capacity could easily double, and perhaps triple, with sufficient foreign investment.[4]

Several states in the region, including Saudi Arabia and Iraq, have exceptionally low production costs for extracting oil, allowing them to make a profit even if the price of oil plunges.[5] Indeed, because extraction costs are higher everywhere else in the world, the share of the world market that Saudi Arabia and Iraq will enjoy is likely to be far higher if the global price of oil is low.[6]

Even limited instability in the oil market presents daunting problems for industrial economies. Because it is hard to substitute other commodities for oil quickly, oil demand declines slowly even in response to exceptionally high prices. Oil prices skyrocketed 400 per-

---

[3]"BP Amoco Statistical Review of World Energy 2000," available at http://www. bpamaco.com/worldenergy/oil (accessed on March 5, 2001).

[4]Although the potential remains for other parts of the world to develop large reserves, many of these regions are plagued with problems that may prevent the full exploitation of these resources. The Caspian region's estimate of known reserves is roughly comparable to those in the North Sea. Developing this energy, however, remains problematic. Russia repeatedly interferes with international oil companies' attempts to sign agreements to export from and invest in Central Asia and often forces the Central Asians to allocate energy to the states of the former Soviet Union at below-market prices. Political turmoil, poor maintenance, and corruption also interfere with attempts to develop Central Asia as a rival to the Gulf. The South China Sea and the Tarim Basin also contain considerable reserves, though it appears that China may have exaggerated the initial findings. Much of the South China Sea reserves are in areas disputed among China, Taiwan, Vietnam, the Philippines, Malaysia, and Brunei. Because of these disputes, the size of the reserves and the cost of retrieving the oil remain uncertain.

[5]http://www.eia.doe.gov/cabs/saudi2.html; http://www.eia.doe.gov/emeu/cabs/iraq.html; and http://www.eia.doe.gov/emeu/cabs/iran.html.

[6]The Gulf also has tremendous natural gas reserves. At the end of 1999, Iran possessed over 15 percent of the world's total share of proven gas reserves, while Qatar, Saudi Arabia, and the UAE control just under 15 percent. "BP Amoco Statistical Review of World Energy 2000," available at http://www.bpamaco.com/worldenergy/naturalgas.

cent in 1973 and increased 150 percent and 50 percent respectively in 1979 and 1990. Switching energy sources or reducing the use of energy is difficult and takes time, making short-term disruptions of vital consequence.[7] For example, if a crisis in the Middle East resulted in a net shortfall of four million barrels of oil per day—around 6 percent of the world's total consumption—it might cause the price of oil to double in the short term, leading to disruption and possible stagnation among leading advanced industrial economies.[8] Oil shocks today, however, are less likely than in the past to cause tremendous disruption because of greater market efficiency, producer desires to create a stable market, latent production potential from developed sources that are not tapped as a result of the high cost of extraction, and government-held reserves.

In addition to ensuring the flow of oil from the Gulf region, the United States also has an interest in preventing, or at least managing, the spread of WMD. Their spread or use is opposed by the United States more generally, even if they do not pose an immediate threat to U.S. interests. Those weapons in the Gulf region pose a threat to U.S. partners and U.S. forces. As discussed in greater detail below, the Gulf region appears especially prone to WMD proliferation, and perhaps even use. The Iran-Iraq war witnessed the repeated use of chemical weapons by Iraq and their occasional use by Iran. Iraq also possessed a vast biological weapons program and came close to developing a nuclear weapon, but the Persian Gulf War and subsequent sanctions and inspection regimes cut these activities short. Iran has pursued nuclear and biological weapons, although its programs lag behind those of Iraq.

The United States also seeks to ensure the security of friendly regimes. In the last decade, the United States has developed strong and close relations to Saudi Arabia, Kuwait, the UAE, Bahrain, Qatar,

---

[7]Steven R. David, "Saving America from the Coming Civil Wars," *Foreign Affairs*, Vol. 78, No. 1, January/February 1999, p. 112.

[8]For total global consumption patterns, see http://www.eia.doe.gov/pub/oil_gas/petroleum/analysis_publications/oil_market_basics/default.htm. For an explanation of the economic impact of an oil price spike, see Edward R. Fried and Philip H. Trezise, *Oil Security: Retrospect and Prospect*, Brookings Institution, Washington, D.C., 1993, pp. 3, 76–77. A rise in the price of oil simultaneously creates recessionary and inflationary pressures, posing a particularly difficult set of problems for policymakers to overcome.

and Oman.[9] Although these states' possession of, or proximity to, large oil reserves was the initial reason for U.S. efforts to build ties, these relations have taken on a life of their own. It is not clear if the United States would intervene with its own forces to keep these regimes in power (in spite of much hand-wringing, Washington did not intervene after revolution toppled the Shah of Iran). However, the United States would almost certainly view any significant political change with concern and in general it favors the status quo.

Finally, the United States' broad, worldwide interest in democracy and human rights has implications for U.S. actions in the Gulf region, although this interest is honored more in the breach. Saudi Arabia, for example, has no free press or free elections, and Saudi women face a variety of restrictions on their travel, employment, and daily lives. Even Kuwait, perhaps the most democratic of the Gulf states, has a limit on who can vote, a ban on political parties, and other basic impediments to democracy.[10] These restrictions elicit only mild criticism from Washington. As Jon Alterman notes, "American officials have tended to accede to official requests to downplay calls for democratization and to shun extensive contacts with those working against the ruling governments."[11]

Concerns over democratization and human rights, however, often limit U.S. actions and could affect the type of support it would provide in a crisis. For example, if unrest in a Gulf state led to mass

---

[9]Many of these relationships became close well before 1990. The United States established a defense cooperation agreement with Oman in 1980. Well before that, the United States had an unwritten "handshake agreement" with Saudi Arabia, with U.S. forces committed to defending the Kingdom's security. See William Quandt, *Saudi Arabia in the 1980s: Foreign Policy, Security, and Oil*, The Brookings Institution, Washington, D.C., 1981; Joseph A. Kechichian, *Oman and the World: The Emergence of an Independent Foreign Policy*, RAND, MR-680-RC, 1995, pp. 139–158; and Nadav Safran, *Saudi Arabia: The Ceaseless Quest for Security*, Cornell University Press, Ithaca, NY, 1988.

[10]See Nora Bensahel, "Political Reform in the Middle East," in Nora Bensahel and Daniel Byman (eds.), *Security Trends in the Middle East and Their Implications for the United States*, RAND, forthcoming.

[11]Jon Alterman, "The Gulf States and the American Umbrella," *Middle East Review of International Affairs*, Vol. 4, No. 4, December 2000, electronic version. Reports that the U.S. State Department was preparing a new program to promote political, economic, and social reform (Peter Slevin and Glenn Kessler, "U.S. to Seek Mideast Reforms; Programs Aim to Foster Democracy, Education, Markets," *Washington Post*, August 21, 2002) in the region appeared too late for evaluation in this study.

demonstrations and the government responded by killing large numbers of unarmed protesters, the United States would have to reconsider arms sales to the country and might otherwise limit ties at least temporarily. In addition, even if unrest threatened the flow of oil or the stability of a friendly regime, it is highly unlikely that the United States would use its own forces to directly assist a regime responsible for torture, arbitrary arrests, and other forms of repression widely condemned in the United States and the West in general. Thus, human rights and democratization goals may inhibit U.S. attempts to defend its other interests.

POTENTIAL THREATS TO INTERESTS

In recent decades, several different types of threats to U.S. interests have emerged. Examples are presented in Table 1.1.

Table 1.1

Past Challenges to U.S. Interests in the Gulf

External Aggression	External Subversion or Terrorism	Internal Unrest
Iraqi invasion of Kuwait (1990)	Iranian support for Shi'a radicals in the Gulf (ongoing, particularly in the 1980s)	Radical seizure of the Grand Mosque in Mecca (1979)
Iranian and Iraqi attacks on Gulf tankers during the Iran-Iraq war (1987–1988)	Iranian support for 1981 coup attempt in Bahrain	Shi'a riots in Bahrain, Kuwait, and the Eastern Province of Saudi Arabia (1979–1981)
Iraqi threats to Kuwait (1994)	Iranian efforts to capitalize on Shi'a unrest in Bahrain (1994–1996)	Radical attacks on U.S. forces in Saudi Arabia (1995)
Iranian and Iraqi WMD programs (ongoing); Iranian seizure of Gulf islands claimed by the UAE (1971 and 1992)	Iranian-affiliated radicals' attempts to assassinate the Emir of Kuwait (1985) and terrorist attacks in Kuwait City (1983)	Shi'a unrest in Bahrain (1994–1996)
	Iranian-backed unrest at the *hajj*	

The greatest danger in the past was outright aggression by Iran or Iraq. In the 1970s, the two states fought a proxy war over the Shatt al-Arab waterway. Iran and Iraq fought a brutal eight-year war with each other in the 1980s, leading to disruptions in the flow of oil and destabilizing the region. Relations in the 1990s remained tense— both sides supported terrorists in the other's country and otherwise sought to destabilize each other.

Iran and Iraq have threatened U.S partners in the Gulf as well as each other. Iraq invaded Kuwait in 1990 and was only expelled by the U.S.-led coalition's massive military effort. Since then, Iraq has repeated its view that Kuwait is an integral part of Iraq. Baghdad has built up troops near the Kuwait border and made numerous threats against Kuwait, Saudi Arabia, and other regional states.[12]

Iran, particularly in recent years, has been less threatening to the Gulf states than Iraq, but nevertheless has regularly shown aggressive intentions. In 1971, Iran occupied several islands claimed by the UAE. After the Iranian revolution in 1979, Iranian leaders regularly called for the overthrow of Gulf rulers. Tehran backed a coup attempt in Bahrain and supported terrorism in Kuwait and Saudi Arabia.

In its war with Iraq, Iran tried to coerce Kuwait and other regional states into halting their support for Iraq by attacking their shipping, particularly their oil tankers. During the anti-regime demonstrations in Bahrain between 1994 and 1996, Iran tried to take advantage of the unrest by training and supporting Shi'a radicals. Since the mid-1990s, however, Iran has toned down its rhetoric toward its Gulf neighbors and sought to improve ties.

Internal instability also poses a threat to U.S. interests. Political Islam has led to violence in the past, particularly in Saudi Arabia. In 1979, Saudi and other Arab religious extremists seized the Grand Mosque in Mecca, holding off Saudi security forces for two weeks. Angered by long-standing discrimination and inspired by the Iranian revolution, Shi'a in Bahrain, Kuwait, and Saudi Arabia rioted against their governments in the early 1980s. In 1995, Islamists destroyed

---

[12]For a review, see Daniel Byman and Matthew Waxman, *Confronting Iraq: U.S. Policy and the Use of Force Since the Gulf War*, RAND, MR-1146-OSD, 2000.

the Office of Personnel Management/Saudi Arabian National Guard office in Riyadh, killing seven, including five Americans.[13] Bahrain suffered widespread rioting and unrest in the mid-1990s, when Bahraini Shi'a protested against discrimination and demanded a greater voice in decisionmaking. Saudi nationals have been a major component of al-Qaeda, as well as a source of financial support to a range of other anti-U.S. Islamist causes. As discussed in Chapter Three, the potential for similar unrest in the coming decade is considerable. In general, many of the Gulf states face economic problems and rising expectations, and have few institutions for incorporating public sentiment into decisionmaking.

This report finds that several types of threats have diminished in recent years while others remain acute. In particular, conventional military aggression by Iraq or Iran appears highly unlikely as long as U.S. forces are in the region. Foreign-backed subversion also is less of a concern. Internal unrest, however, remains a problem—one that could be exacerbated by the presence of U.S. military forces.

STRUCTURE AND RESEARCH APPROACH

This report attempts to anticipate likely challenges to U.S. interests in the Gulf region in the coming decade. To this end, it evaluates various threats to U.S. interests, describing their current status and how they might evolve. In particular, the report explores the military strength of Iran and Iraq, the potential for subversion, and the social and economic weaknesses of all the regional states. In addition, it seeks to identify key uncertainties—such as the price of oil and the potential for dramatic regime change in Iran or Iraq—that may have an important impact.

This report uses several sources and techniques in its findings. First, it draws on interviews conducted in the Gulf region during 1999 and 2000 that covered a range of topics, particularly military readiness and regime stability. Among those interviewed were Gulf businessmen, military and political officials, and U.S. military and diplomatic officials. Second, it uses available primary information, particularly

---

[13]Responsibility remains unclear for the 1996 attack on the U.S. military's Khobar Towers facility in Saudi Arabia, which killed 19 Americans.

economic data, when possible. Third, it employs secondary sources on the region. Fourth, many of these judgments were checked against the opinions of other regional experts.

Chapter Two

THE DECLINING CONVENTIONAL THREAT FROM IRAN AND IRAQ

The possibility of an Iranian or Iraqi attack on U.S. partners in the Gulf has dominated U.S. military planning for the Gulf region since the 1990 Iraqi invasion of Kuwait. U.S. concern about Iranian-backed subversion or terrorism is of even longer duration, dating to the aftermath of the 1979 Iranian revolution. This chapter assesses the conventional military threat from Iran and Iraq and then examines the potential for Iran or Iraq to subvert Gulf governments.

Baghdad's ambitions are expansive, although Iraq currently lacks the military capabilities to achieve them. Saddam Husayn's regime appears committed to gaining regional hegemony and, if possible, regaining control over Kuwait. In addition to invading Kuwait in 1990, Baghdad built up forces along Kuwait's border in 1994 and has repeatedly issued threats against Kuwait in the face of international condemnation. Nor are Iraq's aggressive intentions necessarily unique to Saddam's regime. After Kuwait's independence in 1961, Iraqi Prime Minister 'Abd al-Karim Qasim claimed Kuwait as part of Iraq, foreshadowing the claims Saddam made almost 30 years later.[1]

Iran, for its part, has proven only slightly less aggressive in the last three decades. Under the Shah, Iran seized the islands of Abu Musa and the Greater and Lesser Tunbs, which are claimed by the UAE.[2]

---

[1]Phebe Marr, *The Modern History of Iraq*, Westview Press, Boulder, CO, 1985, pp. 180–181.

[2]Abu Musa is claimed by the emirate of Sharjah; the Tunbs are claimed by Ras al-Khaymah.

After the 1979 Islamic revolution, Iran repeatedly issued threats against the Gulf states, with one Iranian leader claiming that Bahrain was rightfully part of Iran.[3] In 1987–1988, Iran also targeted the shipping, and, in a few instances, the territory, of U.S. partners to punish them for supporting Iraq in its war with Iran. In addition to outright military pressure, Tehran regularly supported Shi'a radicals against the Gulf regimes.

The conventional military threat that Iran and Iraq pose to the region, however, has diminished in the last decade. Although both countries' militaries remain larger and more capable in general than those of U.S. Gulf partners, and their WMD ambitions are particularly troubling, in general the conventional balance has shifted markedly in favor of U.S. partners in the last decade. Indeed, this shift in the balance of forces becomes a remarkable imbalance in favor of the Gulf states when U.S. forces are taken into account. In addition, Iran's ability and inclination to subvert Gulf governments has declined, reducing another potential threat to the Gulf regimes.

THE SHIFTING MILITARY BALANCE

Both Iran and Iraq are relatively weak by historical standards, while the Gulf states have grown stronger. In addition, the considerable U.S. presence has greatly altered the regional balance in favor of U.S. partners. Without U.S. forces in the region, Iraq would still pose a serious threat to the security of U.S. regional partners, while Iran's threat would be real but limited becauser of the difficulty of conducting operations across the Gulf. With U.S. forces in the region, however, the conventional military threat potential aggressors pose is limited.

Iraq's Limited Conventional Military Capabilities

Iraq's military is far weaker in both absolute and relative terms than it was in 1990. Iraqi forces have never recovered from the battering they took from the U.S.-led coalition in Operation Desert Storm.

---

[3]Lenore Martin, *The Unstable Gulf: Threats from Within*, Lexington Books, Lexington, MA, 1984, p. 48.

Coalition forces destroyed, or Iraqi forces abandoned, over 2600 tanks, 1600 armored personnel carriers (APCs), and 2000 artillery pieces. Republican Guard units, the best armed of all the Iraqi military forces, lost roughly half of their heavy equipment.[4]

As a result of sanctions, Iraq has not imported significant numbers of weapons or upgraded existing systems despite its losses in the Gulf War. In addition, UN control over official Iraqi spending has prevented Baghdad from directing its limited budget toward military purchases. For most of the decade, this revenue represented roughly $1 billion per year—hardly enough to rebuild Iraq's forces, let alone expand them, even if the regime could smuggle in larger shipments.[5] Although smuggling and other illegal means have allowed Iraq to acquire some foreign-made spare parts, the regime has not been able to make large-scale purchases.[6] Iraqi arms imports since 1992 total only about $380 million. As of January 1, 2001, Iraq's "arms deficit"— an estimate of the cumulative shortfall in the amount of money required merely to maintain its post–Gulf War force—exceeded $16 billion.[7]

Iraq also has relied on a wide range of suppliers, making it particularly difficult to acquire spare parts needed to ensure readiness. The Iraqi inventory includes systems from the former Soviet bloc, France, the United States, and other countries. (See Table 2.1.)

International sanctions have prevented Iraq from using overseas maintenance facilities for repair or overhaul. Foreign technicians are no longer available to provide maintenance and Iraq has not been able to replenish its parts and supplies. Iraq has long favored combat arms while neglecting maintenance.[8] Not surprisingly, the condition

---

[4]Eliot Cohen (ed.), *Gulf War Air Power Survey*, Vol. 2, Office of the Secretary of the Air Force, Washington, D.C., 1993, pp. 259–261.

[5]Betsy Pisik, "Iraqi Trade Doing Fine Despite Sanctions," *Washington Times*, October 25, 2000, p. 1.

[6]One recent report noted that the Iraqi intelligence service has been trying to buy spare parts on the black market even for its T-55 tanks.

[7]Anthony H. Cordesman, *If We Fight Iraq: Iraq and the Conventional Military Balance*, Center for Strategic and International Studies, Washington, D.C., January 31, 2002, p. 40.

[8]Kenneth Pollack, "The Influence of Arab Culture on Arab Military Effectiveness," unpublished dissertation, Cambridge, MA, 1996, pp. 329, 350–351.

Table 2.1

Origins of Iraqi Military Platforms

Supplier	Main Battle Tank (MBT)	APC	Combat Aircraft (Rotary)	Combat Aircraft (Fixed-Wing)
United States	M-60A1	M-113A1/A2		
Russia/Former	T-72	BTR-50/60/152	Mi-24	MiG 21/23/25/29
Soviet Union	T-62	MT-LB		Su-20/22/24D/25
(FSU)				
France		Panhard M-3	SA 316/321/342	Mirage F-1
China	Type-59			
Czech Republic		OT-62/64		
Brazil		EE-3 *Urutu*		

SOURCE: International Institute of Strategic Studies, *The Military Balance, 2000–2001*, London, 2001 (equipment of U.S. origin is more than a decade old).

of Iraq's aviation assets is poor. Estimates, for instance, suggest that the serviceability of fixed-wing aircraft is about 50 percent; helicopter serviceability is less well known.[9] (Serviceability is the number of platforms ready for combat use with minor or no repair.)

Training, never the Iraqi military's forte, has been further limited for budget reasons. Few pilots have had any but the most basic instruction; a 2000 estimate suggested that senior pilots received 90 to 120 flying hours per year, while junior pilots received only 20.[10] Nor has Iraq been able to exercise large formations with any regularity.[11]

As a result, the Iraqi military is a somewhat motley force of unknown combat strength. Two-thirds of the army's 2200 main battle tanks are obsolete T-55s, T-62s, M-48s, M-60s, and a variety of other models. Most of Iraq's modern armor—as well as other advanced equipment—is apportioned to elite Republican Guard units, leaving the

---

[9]International Institute of Strategic Studies, *The Military Balance, 1999–2000*, London, p. 134; Anthony H. Cordesman and Ahmed Hashim, *Iraq: Sanctions and Beyond*, Westview Press, Boulder, CO, 1997, p. 259.

[10]Jane's Sentinel Security Assessment, *Iraq—Air Force*, January 9, 2002; International Institute of Strategic Studies, *The Military Balance, 1999–2000*.

[11]Andrew Cockburn and Patrick Cockburn, *Out of the Ashes: The Resurrection of Saddam Hussein*, HarperCollins, New York, 1999, pp. 218–230; and Amatzia Baram, *Building Toward Crises: Saddam Hussein's Strategy for Survival*, Washington Institute for Near East Policy, Washington, D.C., 1998, pp. 45–49.

majority of army units poorly supplied. One-third of Iraq's 318 combat aircraft are obsolete MiG 21s, 23s and F-7s.[12]

Many nonquantifiable aspects of military readiness suggest that Iraqi forces are in a poor state. Although information is scarce, morale is probably low. Repeated purges, limited budgets, and the general deterioration of the military forces—once the strongest in the Arab world—have almost certainly undermined morale, a trend that is particularly pronounced outside of the Republican Guard.[13] Since the end of the Gulf War, military officers have attempted at least three coups, suggesting continued dissatisfaction with the regime.

Iraq also suffers from several problems that are not directly linked to the Gulf War and Iraq's subsequent isolation. Iraqi pilots in general have not been encouraged to be flexible or aggressive, so that they do not exploit the aircraft they possess. Iraqi noncommissioned officers do not exercise the leadership common in Western armies. Officers are often discouraged from showing initiative.[14]

In addition, Iraq's military remains heavily politicized, greatly decreasing its overall effectiveness. After the Gulf War and the subsequent anti-regime revolts in the north and south, Iraq purged or shot thousands of officers; such purges have been common in recent Iraqi history.[15] Further, the regime has ideological commissars who operate at all levels of the military to ensure loyalty to the Baath regime. Generals are rotated frequently to ensure that none entrench his position.

This atmosphere of fear and suspicion has a pernicious effect on the military. Promotion is often based more on political connections than on competence. Key decisions, such as when to begin a major operation or to retreat, are often made by a few political leaders with

---

[12]Cordesman, *If We Fight Iraq.*

[13]See, for example, Julian Borger, "Iraq Rearming for War, Say Defectors," *The Guardian,* April 29, 2002.

[14]Cordesman and Hashim, *Iraq,* p. 259; Pollack, "The Influence of Arab Culture on Arab Military Effectiveness," pp. 267–358.

[15]Michael Eisenstadt, "Recent Changes in Saddam's Inner Circle: Cracks in the Wall?" *Policywatch* 22, November 22, 1991, pp. 1–2.

no input from the military.[16] Dissenting opinion, particularly if it has the potential to embarrass Iraq's political leadership, is strongly discouraged. Iraq's chain of command is confused, with multiple militaries and services having similar responsibilities. Even more important, the heavy politicization has undermined morale and professionalism.[17]

As a result, it is questionable whether Iraq can initiate, let alone sustain, conventional operations involving more than a few divisions. However, given the proximity of Kuwait to Iraq, the small size of Kuwaiti forces, and the favorable terrain, Iraq could overrun Kuwait if U.S. forces were not present (see Table 2.2). Iraq could also deploy several divisions against other neighboring states (Jordan, Syria, Iran, and Turkey), although these countries have strong enough militaries to resist Iraq.

The Uncertain Future of Sanctions

Iraq's ability to rebuild its military forces and revitalize its economy depends heavily on whether sanctions are lifted and what, if any, restrictions remain on the regime. Since 1990, Iraq has suffered an array of sanctions that control what Baghdad can purchase. It directs part of its revenue to the autonomous Kurdish north and to Kuwait for reparations. Blame for the sanctions' continuation lies on Saddam's shoulders, and even under sanctions his regime could have taken many steps to alleviate the humanitarian impact.[18] That said, it is undeniable that sanctions, combined with Iraq's poor

---

[16]For example, the decision to invade Kuwait in 1990 was made almost entirely by political leaders, with little military input. During the Iran-Iraq war, Saddam personally ordered disastrous decisions, such as maintaining an exposed position at Mehran that led to heavy Iraqi casualties and the loss of territory. Fred Axelgard, "Iraq and the War with Iran," *Current History*, February 1987, p. 61. For a discussion of the trend of the politicization of militaries throughout the region, see Risa Brooks, "Civil-Military Relations in the Middle East," in Nora Bensahel and Daniel Byman (eds.), *Security Trends in the Middle East and Their Implications for the United States*, RAND, forthcoming.

[17]Andrew Parasiliti and Sinan Antoon, "Friends in Need, Foes to Heed: The Iraqi Military in Politics," *Middle East Policy*, Vol. 7, No. 4, October 2000, pp. 134–138.

[18]Obvious examples include accepting the "oil for food" arrangement, which was proposed in 1991 but accepted only in 1996, and requesting the UN to approve a greater number of contracts for food and medicine.

Table 2.2
Iraqi and Kuwaiti Military Assets

Country	Size of Army	Combat Units	MBT	Quality Active MBT	Ground Combat Vehicles	Self-Propelled Artillery	Towed Artillery	Multiple-Launch Rocket System	Combat Aircraft	Quality Combat Aircraft	Combat Air Squadrons
Iraq	325,000 army 140,000 Republican Guard	3 Armd Div 11 Inf Div 3 Mech Div 7 RG Div	2200	700	6600	150	1800	150	310	112	17
Kuwait	11,000 army	3 Armd Bde 2 Mech Bde	385	293	748	59	0	27	48	48	4

SOURCES: IISS, *The Military Balance, 2000–2001*; Jane's Sentinel Security Assessments, *Iraq—Air Force*, January 9, 2002.

NOTE: The figures assume equal maintenance of Iraqi and Kuwaiti equipment, almost certainly not the case in reality. Iraqi fixed-wing aircraft are reported to be at 50 percent serviceability (IISS, *The Military Balance, 2000–2001*) and rotary-wing aircraft at unknown levels of serviceability. One 2001 report suggested that of Iraq's 2200 MBTs, only 1000 are operational "with about 30% out of service at any time," with APCs available in the same proportion. (Sean Boyne and Salameh Nematt, "Baghdad Resurgent," *Jane's Defence Weekly*, July 25, 2001.) The figures for Kuwait's quality "active" MBTs omit the nearly 100 M1A3 MBTs remaining in storage.

overall economic management, have shattered the country's economy, leading to the destruction of the formal economy and the creation of an economic mafia enriched by smuggling and preferential access to the regime.[19]

The international community, including the United States, is reviewing the sanctions, and it appears likely that they will be loosened in the coming years. On May 14, 2002, the UN Security Council significantly overhauled the sanctions regime, creating a list of military and dual-use items that are restricted but otherwise opening the way for the increased import of humanitarian and civilian goods; the new regime was scheduled to be implemented between May and July 2002.[20] Meanwhile, the ceiling on the amount of oil Iraq can export has been lifted, greatly increasing the revenue available to Iraq (although the UN still must approve all Iraqi purchases). Far more countries appear willing to trade with Baghdad. Iraq has publicized the suffering of the Iraqi people, blaming sanctions for their misery— a perception that, regardless of who is truly culpable, is widely accepted. Sanctions have come under wide criticism, particularly in the Arab world but also in Europe, for their humanitarian impact. At the very least, it is likely that the Iraqi regime will regain control of its oil revenues from the UN and restrictions on dual-use items are likely to be reduced.[21]

Lifting sanctions will benefit Iraq in general, but there are drawbacks from Baghdad's perspective. The regime will have more money to spend, enabling it to co-opt larger segments of the population. Restoring Iraq's economy, however, will require rooting out an en-

---

[19]Sanctions have led to a profound health crisis in Iraq. The "oil for food" arrangement authorized under UN Security Council Resolution 986 mitigated many of the basic nutrition problems Iraqis suffered in the initial years of sanctions. Nevertheless, the quality of health care has declined significantly since before the Gulf War. Among other problems, malnutrition is common, drinking water is often not safe, and sewage systems are in poor repair. See W. Kreisel, "Health Situation in Iraq," testimony presented at the European Union Committee on Foreign Affairs, Human Rights, Common Security, and Defense Policy, Brussels, Belgium, February 26, 2001, electronic version.

[20]Colum Lynch, "UN Council Approves Revision of Iraqi Sanctions," *Washington Post*, May 14, 2002.

[21]Colin L. Powell, "Opening Statement Before the Senate Foreign Relations Committee," March 8, 2001.

trenched black market as well as encouraging the renewal of the private sector. In addition, the Iraqi regime has blamed sanctions for all of Iraq's problems—their removal will expose Iraq's economic mismanagement, corruption, and other problems.[22] As Isam al-Khafaji notes, "Gulf War smoke and a decade of sanctions have masked the fact that Iraq has been heading toward a socioeconomic crisis."[23]

Limited sanctions that affect only military items would still have a profound impact on the region's military balance. The Baath regime has proven able to acquire televisions, washing machines, and other consumer goods, but smuggling in large numbers of main battle tanks or missile launchers is an almost impossible task. Opponents of sanctions such as France and Russia base their criticism on the suffering caused by sanctions, not on the merits of the Iraqi regime. U.S. relations with these states would have to sour considerably before they would sell many advanced weapons to Iraq.

Continued Iranian Weakness

Iran poses even less of a conventional military threat to the Gulf states than does Iraq. Although Iran has faced fewer restrictions than has Iraq in the last decade, its initial military position was far weaker. In addition, the capabilities Iran would need to pose a conventional military threat to the Gulf states are far greater because of geography: Iranian forces would have to conduct amphibious operations across the Persian Gulf, go through Iraqi territory, or mount a large-scale airborne assault operation, any of which would be difficult and exponentially more challenging than an Iraqi invasion of Kuwait.

---

[22]The fate of the Iraqi regime remains a tremendously important variable in the oil market. If Saddam is removed from power or if relations with his regime are normalized, investment in Iraq's oil sector could change the entire oil supply picture. Iraq's revenue depends in part on renewing and expanding its 30-year-old oil infrastructure, which requires considerable outside help. Iraq seeks to more than double its overall production in the next decade and, should sanctions be lifted, this objective is quite feasible. James Richard, "New Cohesion in OPEC's Cartel? Pricing and Politics," *Middle East Review of International Affairs*, Vol. 3, No. 2, June 1999, electronic version; Energy Information Administration, *International Energy Outlook 2000*, March 31, 2000, available at http://www.eia.doe.gov/oiaf/ieo.html (accessed January 17, 2001).

[23]Al-Khafaji, "The Myth of Iraqi Exceptionalism," *Middle East Policy*, Vol. 7, No. 4, October 2000, pp. 66–67.

Iran has not fully recovered from the Iran-Iraq war. The war cost Iran hundreds of thousands of casualties, destroying the flower of a generation of youth.[24] During the closing months of the war, Iran lost up to 60 percent of its heavy equipment.[25] Estimates of the economic cost of the war vary widely. Tehran claims that it suffered over a trillion dollars in damages. A more conservative estimate appears to be around $600 billion, a staggering figure for a middle-income state.[26]

The war also had a profound effect on the Iranian psyche. Iran's eventual loss, and the widespread understanding that Iran could have ended the fighting in 1982, contributed to bitterness in Iran.[27] A comparison can be made with post–World War I France: Iranians today lament the waste of the war and view calls for military action with extreme suspicion. As Shahram Chubin notes, as a result of the war the Iranian regime is "no longer able to effectively call upon its populace for crusades and sacrifices, but will have to act more like a normal state."[28] In part because of this popular disillusionment with the use of force, Iran's military and security forces have avoided steps that would involve Iran in a confrontation. In 1998, Iran backed down from a confrontation with the Taliban in Afghanistan after Taliban forces overran Mazar-i Sharif, killed several Iranian dissidents, and massacred many Afghan Shi'a. Iran also backed down from a confrontation with Turkey in July 1999.[29]

---

[24]Estimates of Iranian casualties vary widely. It is probable that over 300,000 Iranians died and over 600,000 were wounded. Elaine Sciolino, *Persian Mirrors: The Elusive Face of Iran*, The Free Press, New York, 2000, p. 179.

[25]Anthony H. Cordesman, *Iran's Military Forces in Transition: Conventional Threats and Weapons*, Praeger, Westport, CT, 1999, p. 23

[26]H. Amirahmadi, "Economic Costs of the War and Reconstruction in Iran," in C. Bina and H. Zangeneh (eds.), *Modern Capitalism and Islamic Ideology in Iran*, St. Martin's Press, New York, 1992, pp. 290–292.

[27]In 1982 Iranian forces had recovered the territory lost in the initial Iraqi invasion of 1980, but Khomeini kept the war going for six more years in the hope of removing Saddam Husayn from power. William Quandt, "The Middle East on the Brink: Prospects for Change," *Middle East Journal*, Vol. 50, No. 1, Winter 1996, p. 13; and R. K. Ramazani, *Revolutionary Iran*, Johns Hopkins Press, Baltimore, MD, 1988, p. 74.

[28]As quoted in Sciolino, *Persian Mirrors*, p. 185.

[29]Iran claims that Turkish troops in July 1999 attacked sites in Iran as part of their anti–Kurdistan Workers' Party (PKK) campaign. Turkey claims that these were sites in northern Iraq and questioned the presence of Iranians there. A joint commission to

It is not likely that Iran's military would be up to the task if the political leadership changed tack and sought to coerce or intimidate its neighbors. Much of Iran's equipment is obsolete. During the 1990s, Iran acquired several hundred T-72 tanks; small numbers of SA-2s, SA-5s, and SA-6s; 30 Su-24 strike aircraft and 60 MiG-29 fighters; 3 *Kilo*-class submarines; and perhaps 50 C-802 antiship cruise missiles.[30] Nevertheless, these acquisitions only scratch the surface of what Iran needs if it seeks to dominate the Gulf militarily or even to defend itself against a resurgent Iraq. Of the over 1000 modern tanks and perhaps 200 aircraft that Iran sought over the last decade, it acquired only 230 and 72, respectively.[31] Many of Iran's systems are older Soviet or Chinese systems. Less than half of Iran's armored forces are equipped with T-72 tanks; the rest rely on far older T-54s or T-55s or even Chieftain Mk 3/5s or M-60A1s. Iran's air defense is antiquated, with SA-7s its primary surface-to-air missile (SAM) system. F-14s and F-4s sold to Iran during the Shah's rule make up much of its air force, although the acquisition of Su-24s and MiG-29s has improved its air posture somewhat.

Iran's military is also plagued by a lack of a dependable supplier—and as a result a reliance on too many suppliers. In the last 25 years, Iran has purchased equipment from the United States, China, Russia, and other countries (see Table 2.3).

Iran has been stymied in its efforts to acquire many advanced systems. U.S. pressure on Russia and former Soviet bloc countries has led those countries to reduce the number of transfers and the type of systems approved.[32] Because Iran lacks a dependable supplier, its

---

discuss security was revitalized and a parliamentary friendship group was created. Iran reassured Turkey that its eastern border would remain safe and secure. See the comments of Hojjat el Eslam Hasan Rowhani, Vice-Speaker of the Majles [parliament], Islamic Republic News Agency (IRNA), BBC ME/3700MED/7, November 24, 1999. See also the brief report on the incident in *Le Monde,* July 20, 1999, p. 7.

[30]Michael Eisenstadt, "The Armed Forces of the Islamic Republic of Iran: An Assessment," *Middle East Review of International Affairs,* Vol. 5, No. 1, December 2000, electronic version; *The Military Balance, 1999–2000,* pp. 132–133. This figure includes Iraqi aircraft sent to Iran for safety during the Persian Gulf War, which Iran never returned.

[31]Eisenstadt, "The Armed Forces of the Islamic Republic of Iran."

[32]"The Iranian Arms Effort," *Gulf States Newsletter,* Vol. 25, No. 634, April 17, 2000, p. 8; Eugene Rumer, *Dangerous Drift: Russia's Middle East Policy,* Washington Institute for Near East Policy, Washington, D.C., 2000, pp. 55–68.

Table 2.3

Origins of Iranian Military Platforms

Supplier	MBT	APC	Combat Aircraft (Rotary)	Combat Aircraft (Fixed-Wing)
United States	M-47/48/60A1	M-113A1/A2	AH-1J CH-47C	F-4/5 F14
Russia/FSU	T-54/55/62/72	BTR – 50/60/152 MTLB		Su-24 MiG-29
China	Type-59			
UK	Chieftain Mk 3/5 Scorpion			

SOURCE: IISS, *The Military Balance, 2000–2001* (U.S.-supplied materiel is more than ten years old).

forces have a hodgepodge of equipment, which makes training, maintenance, and supply difficult.

As with Iraq, Iran's order of battle disguises deeper weaknesses. Most of Iran's units' manpower and equipment are understrength. In addition, Iran has neglected command and control, advanced munitions, and other systems that would greatly improve military coordination and the effectiveness of existing systems. Many of Iran's systems lack spare parts, and there are not enough technical personnel to service weapons.[33]

Although Iran's military is not as politicized as Iraq's is, it is hardly a model of professionalism. Personal ties and loyalty to the regime often matter as much in promotion as military competence. In addition, Iran's military forces are divided between the regular army and the Islamic Revolutionary Guard Corps (IRGC). This IRGC division, which has roots in the early days of Iran's revolution, reduces the chance of a coup. However, it leads to duplication of missions

---

[33]Michael Eisenstadt, *Iranian Military Power: Capabilities and Intentions,* Washington Institute for Near East Policy, Washington, D.C., 1996, p. 44.

and poor coordination, as different forces respond to different chains of command.[34]

Despite Iran's ambitious rhetoric, the country has actually spent little on its military forces in the last decade. Iran has considered purchasing a wide range of systems, but it has only acquired small numbers of advanced aircraft and tanks. The falling price of oil for much of the 1990s and economic stagnation in general have forced Iran to cut its military spending and procurement, leading to steady declines in military spending in the 1990s despite Iran's many military needs.[35] Iran has not invested enough in its military to replace much of its older equipment.[36] Michael Eisenstadt estimates that Iran has acquired less than one-fifth of the tanks and less than half of the combat aircraft and artillery it requires to ensure its security.[37]

Rather than seek to rebuild its forces entirely along past lines, Iran has focused its rebuilding on improving its capabilities against U.S. forces. As such, it has emphasized systems that improve its ability to counter U.S. naval forces and harass Gulf shipping. It has also strengthened its missile forces, which would be useful against both the United States and Iraq, Iran's primary foe. Tehran has not, however, developed a force projection capability, suggesting that it is not seeking to use conventional military aggression as part of its regional strategy.

Even if Iranian leaders favored military aggression, Iran's options are limited. Iran simply does not have the capabilities for sustained amphibious operations across the Persian Gulf.[38] The air supremacy, naval supremacy, and highly skilled units needed for an amphibious assault are lacking. Iran's air force would not be a match for those of

---

[34]For an assessment, see Daniel Byman, Shahram Chubin, Anoushiravan Ehteshami, and Jerrold Green, *Iran's Security Policy in the Post-Revolutionary Era*, RAND, MR-1320-OSD, 2001.

[35]Eisenstadt, "The Armed Forces of the Islamic Republic of Iran"; Cordesman, *Iran's Military Forces in Transition*, p. 42. Iranian defense spending, however, increased by 50 percent in the 2000–2001 fiscal year.

[36]Cordesman, *Iran's Military Forces in Transition,* p. 45.

[37]Eisenstadt, *Iranian Military Power,* p. 36.

[38]Michael Eisenstadt concurs with this assessment; see "The Armed Forces of the Islamic Republic of Iran."

the Gulf states, and its navy would not last long in the face of Gulf state attacks.

Nor does the configuration of forces favor an airborne assault operation. Even assuming the demands of coordination and sustainability could be met, and that such an operation would be unchallenged by the Gulf states' air defenses, Iran has one airborne brigade, with less than 2000 paratroops. Its army aviation component has a greater capacity in rotary-wing aircraft, but would face exponentially greater challenges from air defenses and demands for precision and coordination. Given the real-world constraints of equipment and maintenance on available lift, however, it is unlikely that Iran could deploy more than a battalion of airborne troops in an operation. This number is likely optimistic—even Kuwait City is beyond the range of the CH-47 helicopter, which constitutes nearly half of the rotary-wing airlift in the Iranian force (see Tables 2.4 and 2.5).

Table 2.4

Iranian Air Transport

Lift Platform	Number[a]	Capacity per Platform	Total Possible Capacity	Range (mi)
CH-47 C (rotary)	44	40	1760	115
Bell 214	130	18	2340	299
UH-1N	12	14	168	493

SOURCE: IISS, *The Military Balance, 2000–2001.*

[a]Assuming all are operational. Sources suggest that Iran's rotary-wing aircraft are at 50 percent or less serviceability. See IISS, *The Military Balance, 2000–2001.*

Table 2.5

Distance from Iranian Airfields to Gulf Capitals (mi)

Airbase/ Airfield	Kuwait City	Doha	Abu Dhabi	Riyadh
Vadahti	215	508	659	546
Estahbanat	365	304	323	546
Agha Jari	139	374	520	457
Gach Saran	183	335	461	465

A more realistic but still difficult option for Iran would be to subvert an already unstable Gulf state. Given the general stability of the Gulf regimes today,[39] there are few opportunities for subversion. Gulf security services would probably quickly identify and arrest any Iranian provocateurs, although limited and uncoordinated acts of terror would be well within Iran's reach. As discussed in more detail below, however, discontent in the Gulf may increase on its own, and Iran could arm and train forces to exacerbate any unrest.

Iran could also use its limited forces to temporarily deny commercial shipping access to the Gulf. It could target shipping transiting the Gulf or sabotage harbor facilities. Iran's antiship cruise missiles, *Kilo*-class submarines, and mine warfare (see Table 2.6) would be useful in this regard. That said, closing the Gulf would shut down Iran's own oil exports, so the tactic would be considered only in extreme circumstances. In addition, Iran's attacks on Gulf shipping in 1987–1988 met with disaster. The U.S. Navy destroyed Iran's navy with ease, and Iran's bellicose behavior united international opinion against Tehran.[40] Any threat against Gulf shipping would thus risk military retaliation and would sacrifice the goodwill with Europe, Japan, and the Gulf states that Tehran has cultivated in the last year.

Table 2.6

Iran's Naval Assets

Submarine	Frigate	Mine Warfare	Amphibious	Marines
3 *Kilo* class	3 *Alvand*	2 *Hejaz* (mine layer)	4 *Hengam* (225 troops)	2 brigades (2600)
		4 MCM	3 *Iran Hormuz* (140 troops)	
			2 *Foque* LSL	

SOURCE: IISS, *The Military Balance, 2000–2001*.
NOTE: MCM = Mine Countermeasures Ship; LSL = Landing Ship Logistics.

---

[39]See Daniel Byman and Jerrold Green, *Political Violence and Stability in the States of the Northern Persian Gulf*, RAND, MR-1021-OSD, 1999.

[40]Michael A. Palmer, *Guardians of the Gulf: A History of America's Expanding Role in the Persian Gulf, 1833–1992*, The Free Press, New York, 1992, pp. 128–149.

Finally, Iran could seize an island in the Gulf claimed by a U.S. ally or an offshore oil platform. As it has in the past with Abu Musa and the Greater and Lesser Tunb islands, Iran could make a land grab, using its forces to fend off any Gulf state attempt to recover the island or platform and raising the cost to the United States of doing so. Such an operation would offer Iran only limited benefits while risking U.S. military retaliation and jeopardizing Tehran's relations with all the Gulf states.

THE FUTURE MILITARY THREAT FROM IRAN AND IRAQ: KEY UNCERTAINTIES

Three uncertain factors complicate future assessments of the threat that Iran and Iraq will pose to U.S. partners in the Gulf: the pace of the countries' efforts to rebuild their militaries; the direction their rebuilding will take; and their willingness to pursue weapons of mass destruction.

The Pace of Rebuilding

How quickly Iran and Iraq can rebuild their forces remains an open question. Both countries suffer from massive equipment shortfalls. Both countries would have to acquire large numbers of tanks, aircraft, artillery, and other systems to match the buildup of the Gulf states over the last ten years.

Both Iran and Iraq suffer from barriers that will hinder a military buildup. Both, as noted above, depend on high oil prices. Because both countries have drawn on a variety of suppliers in the past, their systems are often incompatible, and maintenance and training difficulties are considerable. In addition, foreign suppliers must be willing to sell both countries advanced systems. China can supply many basic systems but in general the systems it offers are obsolete and shoddy.[41] European suppliers could offer a wide range of systems, but they are likely to be responsive to U.S. and Gulf state requests not to provide Iran or Iraq with advanced systems.

---

[41]See Daniel Byman and Roger Cliff, *China's Arms Sales: Motivations and Implications*, RAND, MR-1119-AF, 1999, for a review.

Russia therefore remains the key question mark. Its arms industries need the revenue, it is often at odds with the United States, and it has long-standing arms relationships with both Iran and Iraq. Under U.S. pressure, Moscow in 1996 suspended the sale of advanced conventional systems and halted its aid for Iran's civilian nuclear program. During a March 2001 visit, however, Russian officials indicated that they would again begin helping Iran complete the building of several nuclear reactors and resume supplying advanced systems. Although no specific systems were mentioned in official reports, Russian press reports indicate that they may include T-72 tanks, Su-27 and MiG-29 aircraft, and advanced radars.[42]

Any Iranian regime, unlike the regime in Baghdad, will have to balance military ambitions with the wishes of the Iranian people. As noted earlier, there is little popular enthusiasm for military adventurism in Iran today. In addition, any regime that spent heavily on the military would risk neglecting Iran's many pressing economic problems, which have become a central political issue over the last decade. Even if oil prices are high, there is simply not enough money to embark on a massive military buildup and simultaneously fulfill Iran's infrastructure needs, repair its fraying safety net, provide benefits to the many unemployed, and otherwise restore economic health to the country (e.g., as of 1997, over 9000 km of railroad lines—the only links between some remote villages and the rest of Iran—were either under construction or still in study). Public discontent over living standards burst into the open during a series of demonstrations in the middle of a July heat wave two years ago, when poorer Iranians joined students in demonstrations against the regime. Any regime that emphasized guns over butter would risk unpopularity and would be likely to lose influence as a result.

It will be even harder for Iraq than for Iran to overcome the nonquantifiable problems that hinder a rapid increase in military power. As noted in Chapter Two, Iraqi morale is not likely to increase significantly. In addition, the Iraqi military, particularly its air force, requires considerable training. Politicization is likely to remain intense, because the regime fears giving commanders autonomy

---

[42]"Khatami Has Bumpy Trip in Russia," Radio Free Europe/Radio Liberty Iran Report, Vol. 4, No. 11, March 19, 2001, electronic version.

or promoting individuals who enjoy the respect of the rank and file. And it will take Iraq years to assimilate any new military equipment.[43]

The Direction of Any Buildup

Whether Iran and Iraq can rebuild their militaries masks a deeper but perhaps more important question: What direction would this buildup take? Iranian and Iraqi military postures traditionally have focused on each other and are likely to do so in the future. Both militaries emphasized the need for large land forces to defend (or revise) their disputed border. Air forces contributed to this role, whereas naval forces were distinctly less important. Iran and Iraq remain bitter enemies, making it likely that they will continue to direct their military buildups against each other.

A posture based primarily on land forces, however, is less useful against U.S. forces with their qualitative superiority. Large tank forces would be highly vulnerable to U.S. air power and to precision weapons in general.[44] Even if Iran and Iraq acquired more modern Russian aircraft, such as MiG-29s and Su-24s, they probably would lack the airborne early warning capabilities and sophisticated air-to-air munitions of U.S. platforms. More important, Iranian or Iraqi forces would almost certainly not be trained to the level of their U.S. counterparts. As a result, even massive buildups in Iraqi and Iranian land and air forces would not dramatically shift the military balance.

Iran and Iraq, however, could make a number of purchases that would offset U.S. dominance considerably and make it far harder for the United States to overwhelm their forces. Particularly worrisome purchases or developments would include:

---

[43]Indeed, even this assessment is optimistic. Past efforts to use modern systems efficiently have generally failed. Moreover, even the best militaries take years to learn how to maximize the potential of complex systems.

[44]The Iraqi experience at Al-Khafji during the Gulf War, where U.S. air forces disrupted two Iraqi divisions, demonstrates air power's potency against ground targets in open terrain. Since the Gulf War, the United States has made considerable advances in sensors, precision, and command and control, making air power even more lethal. See Benjamin S. Lambeth, *The Transformation of American Air Power*, Cornell University Press, Ithaca, NY, 2000, pp. 121–124.

- Advanced surface-to-air missiles. If Iran or Iraq acquired SA-10, SA-15, or SA-20 SAM systems, and trained properly on their use, U.S. air operations would become far more difficult. These advanced, long-range systems pose a more robust threat—in terms of range and their ability to defeat existing countermeasures—to U.S. aircraft than their predecessors. To minimize losses, U.S. forces would have to use more resources to suppress enemy air defenses, rely more heavily on stealth, operate aerial refueling and airborne reconnaissance and surveillance platforms outside of missile range, and otherwise tread far more cautiously.

- Sophisticated antiship cruise missiles (ASCMs). For Iran in particular, advanced ASCMs would greatly enhance its ability to target U.S. naval forces that sought to keep the Strait of Hormuz open, protect allied shipping, fly sorties from carriers in the Gulf, or otherwise conduct operations. Iran's C-801 and C-802 missiles are vulnerable to interception and, even if they score a hit, pack only a limited punch. Acquiring the SS-N-22 "Sunburn" ASCM, which was designed to overcome U.S. naval defenses, would give Tehran the ability to pose a far greater threat.[45]

- Ballistic missiles with improved guidance. Iran has, and Iraq had, large ballistic missile programs. These inaccurate missiles are used primarily as a terror weapon against cities or other large targets. Should Iran or Iraq improve the precision of their missile forces, however, they might be able to use them to target ports, airfields, or troop concentrations. This would hinder U.S. access to the region and complicate operations during a campaign.[46]

- Capable special operations forces (SOF). Given the imbalance in conventional forces, Iran or Iraq could use highly trained light forces to conduct sabotage, engage in terrorism, or deny the United States access to the region. If adversary SOF could seize or threaten ports and airports, attack U.S. and allied personnel deployed in the theater, or attack Gulf state leaders directly, it

---

[45]The Sunburn's manufacturers suggest that "one to two missiles could cripple a destroyer-sized ship while up to five could sink a 20,000-ton [carrier-sized] vessel." (Periscope Military Database, accessed May 1, 2002.)

[46]For a review of the threat, see John Stillion and David T. Orletsky, *Airbase Vulnerability to Conventional Cruise-Missile and Ballistic-Missile Attacks: Technology, Scenarios, and U.S. Air Force Responses*, RAND, MR-1028-AF, 1999.

could hinder U.S. operations and planning and pose risks to Gulf regimes.

- Smaller numbers of better-trained forces. Iran and Iraq both have large military forces whose duties often include internal policing, building infrastructure, or other activities not directly related to conventional military operations. Typically, their forces have not used equipment effectively or been able to engage in sophisticated operations.[47] Small numbers of better trained forces would be more effective in resisting the U.S. military.

Shifting their posture in the above directions is not likely to enable Iran or Iraq to defeat U.S. forces, but it might deter U.S. involvement or raise costs for the United States. If Tehran or Baghdad carefully picked the timing and issue of the dispute, they might be able to gain a political victory even though their forces in general are outclassed by those of the United States.[48]

A Shift Toward WMD?

The future status of Iran and Iraq's WMD programs is unknown. Predictions made a decade ago that both countries would by now possess nuclear weapons have proven false. That said, both Iran and Iraq have myriad incentives to acquire WMD. Although both countries regularly cite Israel's weapons programs as justification for their own efforts, they would probably seek WMD even if Israel abandoned its nuclear program. Their rivalry with each other, and to a lesser extent their broader quest for regional dominance, is incentive enough. WMD offer considerable power for little cost relative to

---

[47]See Pollack, "The Influence of Arab Culture on Arab Military Effectiveness," for a review.

[48]In the past, Iraq has tried to exploit anti-U.S. sentiment arising from the collapse of the Palestinian-Israeli peace negotiations to improve its standing in the region. Iraq has also at times engaged in anti-U.S. provocations, including minor troop movements, at times when support for the U.S. containment of Iraq in the region and in Europe appeared limited.

conventional weapons. In addition, both countries' leaders probably see WMD as a useful hedge against the United States.[49]

Iran is pursuing WMD, though at a less frenetic pace than Iraq did in the 1980s. Tehran has stockpiled several hundred tons of chemical agents and has weaponized them successfully. Tehran is researching biological weapons and has repeatedly tried to acquire nuclear weapons. It has also tried to improve its indigenous capabilities for producing plutonium or highly enriched uranium. If Iran can divert fissile material, the timeline for developing a nuclear weapon could shorten to as little as a year or two.[50]

Successful production of nuclear weapons, however, may be some years off for Iran—particularly if it is not able to divert fissile material. Tehran is not near the level that Iraq reached before the Gulf war.[51] Budget limits also prevent Iran from making massive investments in WMD. Moreover, Iran is concerned about its international reputation, which would be jeopardized if it flagrantly violated international agreements on nuclear weapons.

Baghdad's WMD status is less certain, but still troubling. The UN Special Commission on Iraq (UNSCOM) and the International Atomic Energy Agency (IAEA) have destroyed or dismantled much of Iraq's nuclear weapons infrastructure between 1991 and 1998. Yet experts disagree on the extent of Iraq's remaining programs and capabilities.[52] It is highly possible that Iraq retains chemical

---

[49]Neil Partrick, "Weapons of Mass Destruction and the Threat to the Gulf," speech given to the Royal United Services Institute Gulf Security Conference 2000 in London, June 2000. Iran almost certainly also sees WMD as increasingly necessary in the face of the growing threat perceived as emerging from Pakistan (Robert J. Einhorn, testimony before the Senate Foreign Relations Committee, October 5, 2000).

[50]Eisenstadt, "The Armed Forces of the Islamic Republic of Iran."

[51]Partrick, "Weapons of Mass Destruction and the Threat to the Gulf."

[52]The last inspections occurred in December 1998, but in fact inspections had been sporadic and limited for over a year before that. Since December 1998, the IAEA has inspected some Iraqi facilities, but these inspections did not involve assessing undeclared facilities—the core of Iraq's programs. Most recently, the former director of Iraq's nuclear weapons program from 1987 to 1990 reported in testimony to the U.S. Senate Foreign Relations Committee that Iraq possessed most of the components for a nuclear device and noted German intelligence reports that Iraq could have a nuclear weapon by 2005. (Paul Richter, "Scientist Warns of Iraq's Nuclear Gains," *Los Angeles Times*, August 1, 2002.)

weapons precursor stocks and production equipment, biological stocks and some munitions, and some nuclear components as well as expertise. In effect, this enables Iraq to rapidly rebuild its programs should sanctions be lifted. It may also allow Baghdad to quickly become a nuclear power if it acquires fissile material. Iraq might also be able to use biological weapons with lethal effect today, although their effective dissemination will be a challenge.[53]

GULF PARTNERS

Strengths

The military balance is increasingly favorable for the United States not only because of the weakness of Iran and Iraq but also because of the increased relative strength of its Gulf partners. Although Iran and Iraq possess advantages in some gross measures of military strength, such as army size or artillery pieces, the combined assets of the Gulf states meet or exceed those of Iran and Iraq in other measures, such as combat aircraft or main battle tanks (see Table 2.7).

Table 2.7

Gross Military Measures for Iran, Iraq, and the Gulf States

Country	Army	MBT	Ground Combat Vehicles	Artillery	Combat Aircraft
Iran	325,000	1,495	2,640	2,794	236
Iraq	375,000	2,200	6,600	2,100	210
Bahrain	8,500	106	517	107	24
Kuwait	11,000	385	748	86	54
Oman	25,000	117	378	120	24
Qatar	8,500	44	328	44	18
UAE	59,000	331	1,509	312	65
Saudi Arabia	75,000	1,055	3,900	450	343
Saudi/Kuwait	86,000	1,440	4,648	536	397
GCC[a] states	187,000	2,038	7,380	1,119	528

SOURCE: IISS, *The Military Balance, 2000–2001.*

[a]Gulf Cooperation Council.

---

[53]Scott Ritter, "The Case for Iraq's Qualitative Disarmament," *Arms Control Today,* June 2000, p. 11; Michael Eisenstadt, *Iraq's Weapons of Mass Destruction (WMD): An Emerging Challenge for the Bush Administration,* Washington Institute for Near East Policy, Washington, D.C., January 26, 2001.

This trend is even more pronounced when considering the effect of modern technologies on the regional balance of power. Given the size of their militaries, the amount of advanced equipment the Gulf states have purchased since the Gulf War is staggering. As Table 2.8 indicates, several Gulf states have bought highly advanced land, sea, and air systems.

This effort has given the Gulf states a growing "quantity of quality" platforms advantage over Iran and Iraq in the region (see Figures 2.1 and 2.2).

A second important factor is the improved air defense in the Gulf region. In 1995, Saudi Arabia completed the $8 billion "Peace Shield" air defense system, linking advanced short-, medium-, and long-range radars to Saudi airborne warning and control systems (AWACS), fighters, and SAM and antiaircraft batteries; it is possible that it will become the foundation for a proposed Gulf-wide air defense system. Kuwait in 1995 established a similar system on a smaller scale, and has expressed interest in linking its early warning system to that of Saudi Arabia. The Omani air force is planning a similar upgrade. In 2001, the GCC states began construction of a joint air defense system—called Hizaam Al Taawun, or "Belt of Cooperation"—linked to each of the individual state's air defense systems.[54]

The Gulf states are at least a generation ahead, if not more, of Iran and Iraq in terms of the quality of their equipment. Even though, as discussed below, their militaries do not perform close to U.S. or Western allied standards, possession of systems that enable them to engage the enemy with more precision, lethality, and speed enhances their overall ability to defend themselves.

This is particularly true regarding most contingencies with Iran. The Gulf states' superb air assets (as seen above), capable naval systems (see Table 2.9), and advanced air defense systems, enable them, without U.S. assistance, to deny Iran the air and sea supremacy it

---

[54]Jane's Sentinel Security Assessment, *Saudi Arabia—Armed Forces,* July 3, 2002.

Table 2.8
Gulf State Selected Military Purchases, 1991–2000

Type	Saudi Arabia	Kuwait	UAE	Bahrain	Qatar	Oman
Land	315 M-1A2s	218 M-1A2 Abrams tanks	390 Leclerc MBTs	60 M-60A3s	10 AMX-30 MBTs	44 Challenger 2 MBTs
Sea	Retrofit existing frigates; acquire 2 Lafayette-class F-3000 frigates	Um Almaradin fast patrol craft	TNC-45 fast attack craft		4 Barzan fast attack craft	80 Piranhas
Air	72 F-15S; 48 Tornado bombers	40 F/AF-18C/D fighter bombers	80 F-16 block 60 fighters; 30 Mirage 2000-9 aircraft; upgrades to 33 other Mirage 2000	10 F-16C/Ds (AMRAAM-equipped)[a]	12 Mirage 2000-5 fighters	Upgrades to Jaguar fighters
Other	20 Patriot (PAC2) SAM units; 12 AH-64 attack helicopters	16 AH-64D attack helicopters	10 AH-64A combat helicopters; acquiring air-launched cruise missiles	Acquiring ATACMS; SAMs; 30 AH-1Es Cobra attack helicopters		Modernizing air defense radar network

SOURCES: IISS, *The Military Balance, 1999–2000*, pp. 124–128; Anthony H. Cordesman, *The Military Balance in the Gulf*, Vols. III and IV, Center for Strategic and International Studies, Washington, D.C., 1998; http://www.fas.org/asmp/profiles/kuwait.htm; http://www.fas.org/asmp/profiles/saudi_arabia.htm.
[a]AMRAAM = Advanced Medium-Range Air-to-Air Missile.

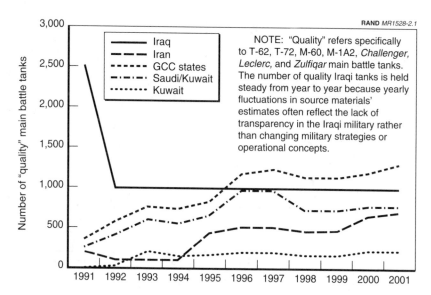

SOURCES: IISS, *The Military Balance, Volumes 1990–1991 through 2000–2001*; and Cordesman, *If We Fight Iraq.*

Figure 2.1—Iraqi, Iranian, and Gulf States' "Quality" Main Battle Tanks

would need to conduct sustained amphibious operations against the Gulf littoral.[55]

The Gulf states have also benefited from closer cooperation with the U.S. military. Increased U.S. training since the end of the Gulf War and regular exercises with the U.S. military have improved the proficiency of Gulf allied forces. U.S. efforts to improve the interoperability of the Gulf militaries and enhance early warning capabilities also improve the Gulf states' ability to defend against Iran or Iraq.[56]

---

[55]If the Gulf states used their systems to full capacity and coordinated their efforts, they could prevent Iran from engaging in all but the most limited hit-and-run operations in the Gulf.

[56]Interviews with U.S. military personnel, May 2000 and February 2001.

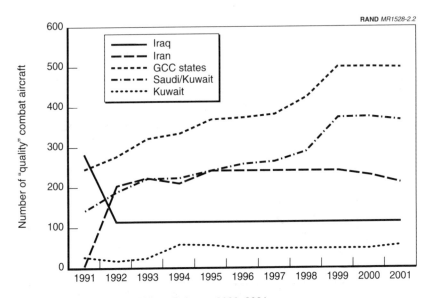

SOURCE: IISS, *The Military Balance, 2000–2001*.

NOTE: "Quality" refers specifically to the following types of fixed-wing aircraft: F-4E, F-5, F-14, F-15, F/A-18, Su-20, Su-224, Su-25, MiG-25, MiG-29, *Hawk* 102, *Hawk* Mk63, and modern *Mirage* and *Tornado* variants.

Figure 2.2—Iraqi, Iranian, and Gulf States' "Quality" Combat Aircraft

Weaknesses

Despite the impressive capabilities of their military systems, the Gulf partners remain dependent on the United States in many contingencies, particularly those involving an Iraqi invasion of Kuwait or Saudi Arabia. Like Iran and Iraq, Saudi Arabia and the other Gulf states have a range of problems that hinder their military effectiveness.[57]

---

[57]Much of this subsection is drawn from an internal report by Nora Bensahel and Daniel Byman, "Improving Engagement with U.S. Partners in the Persian Gulf."

Table 2.9

Naval Surface Assets in the Gulf

Country	Frigates w/SSM	Frigates w/o SSM	Corvettes (SSM)	Missile Craft	Patrol Craft	Patrol Craft Inshore	MW	MCM
Iran	3		2	20	3	38	9	5
Iraq				1		5		2
Bahrain	1	1	2	4		4		
Kuwait				8	2			
Oman			2	4	7			
Qatar				7				
UAE	2		2	8	6			
Saudi Arabia	4		4	9	17			7

SOURCE: IISS, *The Military Balance, 2000–2001.*
NOTE: SSM = Surface-to-Surface Missile, MW = Mine Warfare, MCM = Mine Countermeasures.

Many of the Gulf states face severe manpower shortages because of a small base of eligible recruits. Populations in these states are small to begin with, and as Table 2.10 demonstrates, they often include a high percentage of third-country nationals. Male nationals of military age constitute only a small percentage of the total population, ranging from 12 percent in Qatar and the UAE to 22.3 percent in Saudi Arabia. Military service is not prestigious, and the best recruits often pursue other opportunities.[58]

As a result of these manpower shortages, many of the Gulf states recruit foreign personnel to meet their force goals. More than half of Qatar's military consists of foreign nationals, and the percentages are also high in Bahrain and the UAE.[59] Most of these foreign personnel

---

[58]Interviews with U.S. government and military officials, May 2000.

[59]Qatar actively recruits military personnel in Oman, and as many as 70 percent of Qatari military personnel are Omani and Baluch. This narrows Oman's own recruiting base substantially, forcing the Omani military to rely on foreigners. Approximately 3700 of Oman's 43,500 military personnel are third-country nationals. Anthony H. Cordesman, *Bahrain, Oman, Qatar, and the UAE: Challenges of Security*, Westview Press, Boulder, CO, 1997, pp. 180, 273.

Table 2.10

Population of Eligible Military Recruits

Country	Total Population	Third-Country Nationals as a Percentage of Total Population	Men Aged 13–32 as a Percentage of Total Population
Bahrain	626,000	37	15.5
Kuwait	2,200,000	65	16.4
Oman	2,213,000	27	17.0
Qatar	681,000	75	11.7
Saudi Arabia	18,000,000[a]	27	22.3
UAE	2,650,000	76	11.7

SOURCES: IISS, *The Military Balance, 1999–2000*; CIA *Factbook 1999*.

[a]Most experts interviewed agreed that Saudi population figures are almost certainly exaggerated, perhaps by as much as a third.

come from poorer Islamic states, such as Egypt, Jordan, Pakistan, and Sudan. Foreign contractors provide crucial technical and maintenance support to the Gulf states, since few of these militaries have indigenous support capabilities. Foreign military personnel usually are not as reliable or loyal as nationals. Most regional militaries try to ensure that nationals instead of foreigners staff their elite units, but any major engagement will involve other units as well.

Nor are the Gulf state forces particularly skilled. Regional land forces' maneuver capabilities are poor. Their operational plans have generally been designed for static border defense, so they lack both the equipment and communications assets necessary to go beyond their fixed positions. They also lack effective combined arms and joint capabilities. Moreover, the services do not communicate well with each other, and different elements of single services (e.g., artillery and infantry units) do not coordinate their actions. Neither Saudi Arabia nor Kuwait has demonstrated a capacity for combined arms operations at the brigade level or higher.[60]

Gulf state air forces cannot compensate for the limited numbers and poor skills of the ground forces. Although the Gulf states' air forces are reasonably skilled at air-to-air operations, they have few air-to-

---

[60]Cordesman, *If We Fight Iraq*, p. 2.

ground capabilities. In general, Gulf state air forces do not train on air-to-ground missions. Their platforms do not possess the advanced munitions that would destroy or disrupt advancing enemy armored columns. Interservice communication within country militaries, to say nothing of interservice communication among possible Gulf coalition members, is almost invariably poor, preventing effective air-land coordination. As a result, Gulf air forces could do little to halt a significant invasion. Indeed, the Royal Saudi Air Force's skill levels have declined over the last decade despite considerable government investment. Both the Saudi and Kuwaiti capacity for joint operations remains low.[61]

Gulf militaries are plagued by many of the same problems that Iran and Iraq face. Gulf militaries generally do not train under realistic operational conditions.[62] They tend to spend their procurement dollars on acquiring new and technologically advanced weapon systems instead of developing basic support capabilities. A frequent consequence is the inability to integrate the new, advanced weapon systems into realistic concepts of operation and training activities. For example, more than 100 M-1A1 tanks in Saudi Arabia are warehoused, awaiting trained staff.

The Gulf states generally lack the logistics infrastructure to sustain operations for more than a short time. Preventive maintenance is not emphasized.[63] Finally, the Gulf militaries suffer from problems related to the chain of command. Personal relationships, family ties, and political factors often determine key promotion and staffing decisions. This problem is exacerbated when members of the royal family serve in the military, because ranks do not always correspond to family status.[64]

---

[61]Cordesman, *If We Fight Iraq.*

[62]Pilots are not always required to become instrument rated; the desert skies usually have high visibility and pilots are not required to retest their skills once they have become certified. In Kuwait and Saudi Arabia, land forces generally train for only a few hours every day, avoiding extended hours in the heat. They almost never train in chemical protective gear. Interviews with U.S. government and military officials, May 2000.

[63]Oman, where logistics and maintenance capabilities are emphasized more than elsewhere in the Gulf, is a partial exception to these generalizations. Cordesman, *Bahrain, Oman, Qatar, and the UAE,* pp. 172–196.

[64]Interviews with U.S. government and military officials, May 2000.

Unfortunately, the Gulf states show little sign of pooling their military resources to counter threats from Iran or Iraq. In general, all the regional militaries prefer to work bilaterally with the United States rather than multilaterally. Political disagreements within the GCC have limited military cooperation in the region. The smaller GCC states fear Saudi hegemony and distrust the GCC as a mechanism for resolving bilateral differences. As Simon Henderson notes, "If it [the GCC] had a motto, it would probably be 'caution.'"[65] Personal differences among leaders and minor border disputes also inhibit cooperation.[66]

A chief consequence of these problems is that Saudi Arabia and Kuwait will remain heavily reliant upon U.S. forces in the event of a large land attack by Iraq. Current Kuwaiti defense doctrine accepts and relies upon this fact, stating as its objective the halt of a ground attack for 48 hours, in which time a coalition response can be mobilized.[67]

THE DOMINANT U.S. POSITION

In addition to the greater strength of U.S. partners and the weakness of likely adversaries, the United States has dramatically increased its regional military presence and overall capacity to respond to contingencies. As a result, the Iranian or Iraqi militaries are overmatched and would have relatively few options for aggression as long as U.S. forces in the region can quickly respond to belligerence.

The U.S. presence in the Gulf varies according to rotation schedules and the security situation of the moment, but it has expanded dramatically since before the Gulf War. On average, the United States deploys 25,000 personnel in the Gulf region, as well as an additional 1000 U.S. Air Force (USAF) personnel in Turkey who are responsible for Operation Northern Watch. Currently, U.S. forces include ap-

---

[65]Simon Henderson, *The Gulf Cooperation Council Defense Pact: An Exercise in Ambiguity,* Washington Institute for Near East Policy, Washington, D.C., January 16, 2001, electronic version.

[66]Ghanim Alnajjar, "The GCC and Iraq," *Middle East Policy,* Vol. 7, No. 4, October 2000, p. 92; Henderson, *The Gulf Cooperation Council Defense Pact.*

[67]Jane's World Armies, "Kuwait," Jane's Information Group (www.janes.com), July 17, 2001.

proximately 5000 Army soldiers (manning one heavy brigade) in Kuwait; 5000 USAF personnel largely in Kuwait and Saudi Arabia (home to a U.S.-run Coalition Air Operations Center); and 13,000–15,000 Navy and Marine personnel. Roughly 200 aircraft are in the region, most of which are part of Operations Northern and Southern Watch.[68] There are some 3300 troops in Qatar, mostly at the al-Udeid airbase, which is being developed as a second Coalition Air Operations Center.[69] (All troop deployment numbers in the region are notional and likely to change, given the continuing war on terrorism.)

In addition to the forces it has in the theater, the United States has augmented its cooperation with the Gulf states and its ability to respond rapidly in a host of other ways. Washington has prepositioned U.S. Army mechanized brigade sets, USAF bare-base sets, U.S. Navy forward logistics sets and infrastructure, and other assets in several Gulf countries. The United States was recently reported to have prepositioned equipment for three Army armored brigades and a Marine brigade in the region.[70] Washington is also arranging to preposition large amounts of Army equipment in Qatar, making Camp Snoopy there the largest Army prepositioning site in the world. In addition, the United States has signed defense cooperation agreements with all the Gulf states except for Saudi Arabia.[71] U.S. forces exercise frequently with Gulf state militaries and have an enhanced ability to work with regional partners and use regional facilities with little notice.

The United States has made great strides in the last decade in improving its ability to respond rapidly to a crisis, independent of prepositioning or its forward presence. Advances in targeting, in-

---

[68]Alfred B. Prados, "Saudi Arabia: Post-War Issues and U.S. Relations," *CRS Issue Brief*, December 2, 1996, accessed at http://www.fas.org/man/crs/3-113.htm on March 8, 2001; "U.S. Forces Order of Battle," Federation of American Scientists, available at http://www.fas.org/man/dod-101/ops/iraq_orbat.htm.

[69]Robert Burns, "U.S. Beefs Up Airbase in Qatar," *Associated Press*, July 2, 2002, and Bradley Graham and Thomas Ricks, "Contingency Plan Shifts Saudi Base to Qatar; US Wants to Lessen Dependence on Riyadh," *Washington Post*, April 6, 2002.

[70]Eric Schmitt and Thom Shanker, "American Arsenal in the Mideast Is Being Built Up to Confront Saddam Hussein," *New York Times*, August 19, 2002.

[71]Washington has had a defense agreement with Oman since 1979. The agreements with the other Gulf states were signed in the decade after the Gulf War.

formation processing, and precision munitions enable early arriving aircraft to deliver more and more-lethal strikes than before. As a result, the United States is well prepared to respond to contingencies that would tax in-place assets.[72]

The strong U.S. capabilities do not rule out all adversary options. The use of nuclear weapons, and to a lesser degree biological systems, would change the playing field in the Gulf region considerably. Although Iran and Iraq possess extensive chemical stockpiles, the Iran-Iraq war suggested that neither country used these weapons with remarkable skill. Given U.S. defenses, post–Gulf War preparation for operations in a chemical environment, and the speed of operations, it is not likely that chemical weapons would significantly change the military balance, although they would complicate operations considerably. Nuclear weapons, however, pose a far graver risk, both as a tactical and as a strategic threat. The risk of a nuclear attack on U.S. forces or U.S. partners would raise the risks of any U.S. intervention considerably. As a result, it might embolden U.S. adversaries, making them more likely to consider land grabs or other limited attacks in the hope that their nuclear arsenal would deter the United States from counterattacking with impunity. In some circumstances, biological weapons could also be used as a strategic threat, although the delayed effects of a strike and the weapons' unproven nature make them less effective than nuclear weapons.

Even the tacit threat of using these weapons against the United States, however, poses risks for Iran or Iraq. If Iran or Iraq threatened to use biological or nuclear weapons, the United States might intervene directly given the threat these weapons pose: thus, the supposed deterrent effect of these weapons might instead produce a motive (or, from Tehran or Baghdad's point of view, a pretext) for an attack. In any event, the United States would be likely to elevate counter-proliferation as an objective if military operations were conducted for other reasons (e.g., to enforce no-fly zones over Iraq), perhaps leading to attacks on biological or nuclear facilities.

Beyond WMD, Iraq and Iran would have a free hand in their own countries and might commit acts, such as moving against the Kurds

---

[72]Lambeth, *The Transformation of American Air Power*, pp. 168–169, 297–321.

in northern Iraq, that would bring them into conflict with the United States. Finally, Iraq might be able to conduct a short-notice invasion of Kuwait with two to three divisions that would be difficult for the United States to defeat easily, although over time Iraqi forces would be overwhelmed.

A DECLINE IN SUBVERSION

In addition to a decreased danger of outright invasion, the threat of subversion has also fallen in the last decade and shows little sign of reawakening. In the past, subversion was a potent threat. Although Iraq never managed to inspire Gulf citizens with its message, Iran at times shook the Gulf with its efforts to weaken, subvert, and overthrow the traditional Arab regimes. Iran's appeal was particularly strong to the Gulf's Shi'a Muslims, who constitute roughly 70 percent of Bahrain's population, 25 percent of Kuwait's, and 5 percent of Saudi Arabia's (where they are concentrated in areas such as al-Hasa' Province, where much of Saudi Arabia's oil reserves are located). In Bahrain, Shi'a demonstrations unsettled the island in 1980, and in December 1981 Shi'a conspirators of the Islamic Front for the Liberation of Bahrain tried to overthrow the government—with Iran helping organize the group and offering naval support in the event of a successful coup. Demonstrations took place in Kuwait in response to the Iranian revolution, and Shi'a groups linked to Iran blew up the U.S. Embassy in Kuwait and tried to assassinate the Kuwaiti emir. In Saudi Arabia, rioting broke out in 1979 and 1980 in response to Khomeini's return to Iran and calls for revolution.[73] During much of this time, Khomeini and lesser leaders in Iran regularly called for revolution in the Gulf, denouncing the ruling families as impious, corrupt, and pawns of the West. This revolutionary rhetoric appealed even to nonreligious Shi'a, who keenly felt the discrimination and second-class status they routinely suffered in the Gulf.[74]

The most significant recent involvement of Iran in subversion in the Gulf was its meddling in Bahrain between 1994 and 1996, when rioting and demonstrations were common among Bahraini Shi'a. The

---

[73]Martin, *The Unstable Gulf,* pp. 81–83.

[74]Graham Fuller and Rend Rahim Francke, *The Arab Shi'a: The Forgotten Muslims,* St. Martin's Press, New York, 1999.

causes of the violence were linked to discrimination, corruption, and other problems endemic to Bahrain. Iran, however, tried to create a Bahraini Hezbollah organization, but the Bahraini Security and Information Service quickly suppressed this.[75]

Since that time, Iran has become far less active in promoting unrest in the Gulf. It continues to support terrorists seeking to halt Arab-Israeli peace negotiations and backs anti-regime groups in Turkey and particularly in Iraq. Although information is scarce, it is highly likely that Tehran retains ties to Shi'a radicals and other militants in the Gulf—ties formed from kinship and religious networks and through previous attempts to mobilize local Shi'a and other Muslims. Iran, however, has actively courted the Gulf states in an attempt to improve relations. In part, this effort has resulted from the futility of supporting peoples against governments and Iran's need to cooperate with the Gulf states, particularly Saudi Arabia, in the oil market.

Perhaps most important, the attraction of the Iranian revolution has declined in the Gulf. The death of the charismatic Ayatollah Khomeini, and his replacement by the uninspiring and intellectually second-rate Ayatollah Khamene'i, has cooled the ardor of many Gulf citizens. In addition, cultural differences between the Arab Shi'a of the Gulf and the Persian Shi'a of Iran, the stagnation of the Iranian economy, and the evident discontent that most Iranians today appear to have for their own leadership have made Iran a less attractive model in general. As a result, the appeal of the Iranian revolution has diminished.[76]

The twin threats of conventional military aggression and subversion have both declined in recent years. The possibility of aggression remains real but is more manageable than it was because of a decline in the power of regional adversaries, improved regional partner capabilities, and a far stronger U.S. regional position. Subversion is even less of a concern given Iran's more moderate government and

---

[75]Byman and Green, *Political Violence and Stability*, pp. 33–35. The Iranian-backed Bahraini Hezbollah actively spread propaganda against the Al Khalifa, but the organization was not linked to any actual acts of violence or to the larger demonstrations that occurred. "Bahrain: Defendants' Confessions Reported," Manama WAKH, FBIS-NES-96-110, June 5, 1996; "Bahrain: Interior Ministry on Arrest of 'Hizballah of Bahrain' Group," Manama WAKH, FBIS-NES-96-107, June 3, 1996.

[76]Fuller and Francke, *The Arab Shi'a*, pp. 77–78.

the declining appeal of its message. As discussed in the next chapter, however, threats to U.S. interests remain, particularly in the form of instability among U.S. Gulf partners. Moreover, as Chapter Four indicates, many uncertainties remain that could lead to additional challenges for the United States in the Gulf region.

Chapter Three

INTERNAL THREATS TO REGIONAL PARTNERS

Although the external threats to U.S. interests are limited, the picture is darker when the internal situation of U.S. partners is examined. To be clear: U.S. partners are not on the brink of revolution or dramatic regime change. It is likely, however, that economic and social pressures will grow in the coming decade, making it more difficult for these states to cooperate openly and wholeheartedly with the United States. Iran and Iraq, even more than U.S. partners, face internal threats that could lead to dramatic regime change.

THE FRAYING SOCIAL CONTRACT

A range of economic and social problems is undermining the political arrangement that has governed social relations in the Gulf since the discovery of oil. Gulf governments have not established effective political institutions for managing any increased tension. As a result, governments in the Gulf are under more pressure to be responsive, and the potential for unrest is growing.

Growing Stagnation and Reform

Discontent stemming from economic problems may increase in several Gulf states in the next decade. Despite their countries' oil wealth, citizens in Oman, Bahrain, and Saudi Arabia face a declining standard of living and rising unemployment rates. State-dominated economies, rapid population growth, and a lack of economic diversification will make it difficult for these governments to maintain the cradle-to-grave welfare state that earned them the goodwill of much of their citizenry in the past. In all three of these countries, population growth has averaged over 3 percent per year in the past two decades, greatly straining existing social services and posing an employment problem that would challenge even strong economies.[1] Kuwait, Qatar, and the UAE, on the other hand, have enough energy reserves to maintain a high living standard for their citizens even if energy prices should fall; they are not likely to experience unrest for economic reasons.[2]

Economic Problems Common to the Gulf States

Oil wealth, which led to dramatic standard of living increases in the Gulf for much of the second half of the twentieth century, no longer is enough to ensure the prosperity of several states. Living standards in Saudi Arabia, Bahrain, and Oman have remained at a standstill in recent years. For example, from 1980 to 1998, the Saudi economy grew at an average of 0.2 percent a year—a stagnation that ended only when oil prices soared in 1999 and 2000.[3]

---

[1] For a review of the implications, see Byman and Green, *Political Violence and Stability in the States of the Northern Persian Gulf*, pp. 14–16.

[2] Kuwait and the UAE are also heavily dependent on oil exports, although both countries have offset this dependence through significant investments in "downstream" industries. Oman and Bahrain, which lack large oil reserves, already face economic problems. Qatar enjoys rich natural gas reserves as well as oil deposits. Oil also constitutes the lion's share of Iran's and Iraq's exports and government revenues. See http://www.eia.doe.gov/cabs/saudi2.html and http://www.eia.doe.gov/emeu/cabs/orevcoun.html .

[3] "Can Crown Prince Abdullah Lead His Desert Kingdom into the 21st Century?" *Business Week*, May 21, 2001; United States Embassy in Riyadh, "Saudi Arabia: 2000 Economic Trends," April 2000; Saudi American Bank, "The Saudi Economy: 2001 Performance, 2001 Forecast," p. 1. During this time, real gross domestic product (GDP) growth averaged only 1.9 percent a year. Real GDP, however, does not take into account temporary increases in the price of oil, which can create windfalls. Real gross domestic income (GDI) measures the total income available to the entire economy, both to the government and the private sector. When oil prices are high, real GDP underestimates how well the Saudi economy is doing; when prices are low, it overestimates the strength of the economy. From 1995 to 2000, real GDI grew at an average 6.4 percent, with the year 2000 representing an impressive 20.7 percentage growth. Should the terms of trade shift against Saudi Arabia, real GDI will fall accordingly. See "Special Report on Saudi Arabia," *Middle East Economic Digest*, March 16, 2001, p. 30.

Gulf regimes have failed to diversify their economies beyond the oil sector.[4] Oil dominates the Gulf economies, leaving them vulnerable to sudden price fluctuations. For example, about 40 percent of Saudi Arabia's GDP, and over 90 percent of its export earnings come from oil revenues. Many industries depend heavily on subsidized energy, as well as direct and indirect government subsidies, to survive. As discussed in greater detail in Chapter Four, oil prices are predicted to average around $21 a barrel (in 1998 dollars) in the coming decade— a price that will not bankrupt the Gulf states but will not be enough to solve the economic problems of Saudi Arabia, Bahrain, and Oman in particular.[5]

The Gulf states suffer from a number of weaknesses that inhibit growth outside the oil sector. All the Gulf states spend heavily on government salaries, and investment levels are low compared with other developing economies.[6] The state dominates the economies of most Gulf states. Over half of the workforce in the Gulf is employed directly by the state. Even outside the oil sector, governments often dominate electric companies, hotels, banks, telecommunications, and other sectors.[7]

The remarkable energy reserves in the Gulf have hindered economic diversification in the region. Outside and domestic investment focus first on the energy sector. Moreover, the surge in oil prices led to rapid increases in the prices of nontradable goods, which in turn led local manufacturers and merchants to concentrate on the lucrative

---

[4]For a more comprehensive look at the economic challenges facing states in the region and their likely political consequences and responses, see Alan Richards, "The Political Economy of Economic Reform in the Middle East," in Nora Bensahel and Daniel Byman (eds.), *Security Trends in the Middle East and Their Implications for the United States*, RAND, forthcoming.

[5]This prediction comes from the authors' interviews with executives in the U.S. oil industry and government. It also meshes with the U.S. Department of Energy's "base scenario." See Energy Information Administration, *Annual Energy Outlook 2001*, at http://www.eia.doe.gov/oiaf/aeo/economic.html#international.

[6]Saudi American Bank, "The Saudi Economy," pp. 8–9; "Can Crown Prince Abdullah Lead His Desert Kingdom into the 21st Century?"

[7]F. Gregory Gause III, *Oil Monarchies: Domestic and Security Challenges in the Arab Gulf States*, Council on Foreign Relations Press, New York, 1993, pp. 52–53, 59. Saudi Arabia faces another problem: payment on the debt is crowding out government capital expenditures, which are needed to diversify the economy. United States Embassy in Riyadh, "Saudi Arabia: 2000 Economic Trends."

domestic market rather than on developing industries that were globally competitive. Investments in energy have produced few positive externalities that have encouraged the growth of other sectors of the economy.[8]

Corruption and ruling family involvement in the economy are other problems. Interviews with area businessmen and U.S. officials in the Gulf indicate that connections with the ruling family are often required for any major business. In addition, in Saudi Arabia, royal family members are increasingly demanding a share of private business transactions, whereas previously they had confined their role to the state's oil sector and government-directed activities.[9] Although solid information on the amount spent on the thousands of royal family members is lacking, a common estimate is that each Saudi prince receives about $3000 per month, with senior princes getting far more. Opposition groups, no doubt exaggerating, claim that 40 percent of government revenues go to the royal family.[10] The lack of transparency in the Saudi economy only fuels speculation and conspiracy theories and inhibits foreign investment. Government spending on the royal family, on defense, and on other sensitive matters is seldom revealed.[11]

Education systems in the Gulf are inadequate and do not produce large numbers of skilled workers, although they have advanced from only 30 years ago, when many states lacked a comprehensive education system and much of the populace in the region was illiterate. Moving much beyond basic literacy, however, has proven a difficult step.[12] Moreover, roughly half of Saudi Arabia's graduates have

---

[8]The so-called "Dutch disease" is a common phenomenon in resource-rich economies. In the Gulf, many of the problems inherent in resource-based wealth are magnified by political, demographic, and social weaknesses.

[9]Interviews in Saudi Arabia, May 2000.

[10]"Can Crown Prince Abdullah Lead His Desert Kingdom into the 21st Century?"

[11]For an opposition criticism along these lines, see "The Saudi Economy Crisis: Entrance and Exit," available at http://www.miraserve.com/pressrev/eprev76.htm (downloaded May 23, 2001).

[12]James Placke, "Low Oil Prices: Implications for the Gulf Monarchies," talk at the Washington Institute for Near East Policy, Washington, D.C., July 15, 1998.

degrees in subjects related to the study of Islam, leaving them unprepared for the modern job market. Too often, graduates of Gulf schools are not trained to think critically and are largely innumerate.

The Gulf states also are dependent on expatriate workers. The salaries for menial jobs are low, and many Gulf state citizens consider manual labor to be beneath them. The poor education system, however, has hindered efforts to replace high-skilled foreign labor. As a result, efforts to replace expatriate workers with locals— "Omanization," "Saudization," "Bahrainization," and so on have not occurred at a rapid pace.

As a result of these economic problems, unemployment is growing. Saudi Arabia's unemployment rate is estimated at 14 percent and is steadily increasing. Bahrain and Oman probably suffer similar unemployment rates.[13] Unemployment is likely to increase in the coming years as a result of rapid population growth. Saudi Arabia, Qatar, Oman, and Kuwait all had estimated population growth rates in 2000 of over 3 percent, rates they have sustained for several decades.[14] Over half the Saudi population is under 18. The economy currently creates enough jobs for only 40,000 of the 110,000 who enter the job market each year.[15] Brad Bourland, the chief economist at the Saudi American bank, notes that job creation in Saudi Arabia "has not been keeping up with labour force growth over the past decade."[16] The Kingdom needs a job growth rate of over 6 percent to keep up with its increasing population.[17]

---

[13]http://www.odci.gov/cia/publications/factbook/geos/ba.html#Econ. Information on Gulf employment rates is limited both because of poor government information in general and because there are few incentives for individuals to register as unemployed.

[14]http://www.odci.gov/cia/publications/factbook.

[15]Saudi American Bank, "The Saudi Economy," pp. 2 and 12–13; "Can Crown Prince Abdullah Lead His Desert Kingdom into the 21st Century?"; United States Embassy in Riyadh, "Saudi Arabia: 2000 Economic Trends."

[16]During this time, real GDP averaged only 1.9 percent a year. See "Special Report on Saudi Arabia," p. 30.

[17]United States Embassy in Riyadh, "Saudi Arabia: 2000 Economic Trends."

Limited Momentum for Reform

Several Gulf states are moving fitfully in the direction of economic reform. Bahrain has tried to portray itself as a regional financial center and Oman has tried to encourage foreign investment. Most surprisingly, Saudi Arabia is taking several steps in the right direction. The Saudi government has used the recent boom in oil prices to improve its overall fiscal strength rather than increasing spending. In September 1998, Saudi Arabia invited U.S., and later European, energy companies to submit proposals, reversing years when foreign direct investment in energy was discouraged. In addition, it has adopted a privatization strategy, approved a foreign investment law, opened its stock market to foreign investors, and tried to stimulate tourism, among other changes. It has also taken steps to adhere to World Trade Organization (WTO) regulations and streamline regulations for companies operating in the Kingdom.[18]

How far the Gulf states will go down this path is not clear. The surge in oil prices has reduced the pressure for reform. So far, regional states have not made much of an effort to sell state assets, a key part of any reform. Moreover, state monopolies and many ruling family members with ties to the patronage-driven economy oppose significant change. The thousands of ruling family members also enjoy a range of free or subsidized services, perquisites that will be difficult for rulers to cut.[19]

Impact on the Social Contract?

If reform does not succeed, the social contract in several Gulf states may fray. Even as regional economies have stagnated, the expectations of the citizenry have risen. When oil prices were high, Saudi and other Gulf state leaders forged a bargain with their peoples. The regime would provide a high level of services in exchange for political loyalty, or at least passivity. Governments today, however, cannot

---

[18]Saudi American Bank, "The Saudi Economy," pp. 2, 17–18. The progress of Saudi Arabia toward WTO standards is particularly important, because it will address many of the Kingdom's problems with transparency and a lack of market regulations.

[19]"Can Crown Prince Abdullah Lead His Desert Kingdom into the 21st Century?"; United States Embassy in Riyadh, "Saudi Arabia: 2000 Economic Trends."

provide enough jobs, advanced educational opportunities, or other benefits, and the economies are not diversified enough to offer sufficient opportunities in the private sector.[20]

Gulf youths today expect more from the government than did their parents, even though they are receiving less. Most Gulf residents under the age of 30—easily more than two-thirds of the population— grew up accustomed to a high standard of living. They continue to expect high-quality health care, housing, and other services that their parents never knew as children. Furthermore, many received higher degrees, increasing their ostensible qualifications for high-status, high-paying jobs. As a result, many Gulf residents consider jobs involving physical labor unacceptable and believe it is their right to have an undemanding, high-paying government job. If regimes cannot provide such largesse, the population is likely to be less supportive and more critical. This will make open support for the United States difficult, particularly for unpopular military operations.

HOW THE U.S. PRESENCE AND POLICY INCREASE CHALLENGES

The U.S. military presence and overall policy at times increase domestic criticism of the Gulf regimes. Regional governments support the U.S. presence directly, by providing fuel, supplies, and reimbursements to the United States, and indirectly, by forgoing rent and tax payments. Although the total cost is only around $300 million a year,[21] the *perception* of the cost of the U.S. presence is high. Much of the public in the Gulf believes their governments spend large amounts on supporting U.S. forces (and correctly believe they spend far more on procuring U.S.-origin weapon systems).[22]   One opposi-

---

[20]Joseph Kostiner, "Low Oil Prices: Implications for the Gulf Monarchies," talk at the Washington Institute for Near East Policy, Washington, D.C., July 15, 1998.

[21]United States Secretary of Defense, *Report on Allied Contributions to the Common Defense*, March 2000, pp. III-28 and D-10 through D-12.

[22]Information on public attitudes in the Gulf, particularly in Saudi Arabia, is difficult to obtain. That said, interviews with academics and government and military officials in the region, as well as knowledgeable Americans, suggest widespread public concerns about spending to maintain U.S. forces. Estimates given in interviews run into the tens of billions of dollars a year, far exceeding the actual amount required to maintain the U.S. presence in the region.

tion publication acidly observes, "It is noteworthy that the United States continued to send delegations urging the Kingdom to cut its budget deficit, and then sent others urging the same officials to pay the money owed to arms exporters and other contractors, while continuing to put pressure to win new arms deals. And these are obviously irreconcilable demands."[23]

The large U.S. military presence in the Gulf serves as a constant reminder that the regional states do not possess the military capabilities to defend themselves. It exposes the regional governments to domestic criticism for failing to ensure state security and relying instead on security guarantees from the United States. This criticism is particularly strong in Saudi Arabia, a country whose annual defense budget is almost twice as large as the combined defense budgets of Iran and Iraq.

Depending on foreigners to provide security is particularly problematic because Western political and religious values are often seen as incompatible with Islamic teachings. This perception poses particular problems in Saudi Arabia, whose religious establishment believes that Western values are corrupting and should be kept out of the country, and whose leaders' legitimacy is at least partly based on their status as "guardians of the faith" and protectors of the holy Muslim cities, Mecca and Medina. In Saudi Arabia, even pro-regime religious leaders such as Shaykh 'Abd al-Aziz bin Baz have implicitly criticized Saudi security ties to the United States. The U.S. military presence highlights the erosion of traditional values and institutions. The perception of what the U.S. military presence entails often shapes attitudes. Yusif al-Karadawi, a respected and modern Islamist cleric living in Qatar, argues that the U.S. military presence poses a danger "not just in Qatar, but across the Gulf. You have given money and weapons to Israel at our expense! And everywhere your military goes it has insisted on alcohol, night clubs, discos, and bars. And, in Islam, these things are all very definitely *haraam* [forbidden]."[24]

---

[23]"The Saudi Economy Crisis."

[24]Mary Anne Weaver, "Democracy by Decree," *The New Yorker*, November 20, 2000, p. 59. Of course, U.S. forces in the Gulf face considerable restrictions in their interactions with the local population. Despite the circumspection of U.S. forces, perceptions of licentiousness remain.

OPPOSITION TO U.S. POLICY IN THE MIDDLE EAST

Many U.S. actions in the Middle East are widely unpopular in the Gulf. Most criticism centers on the staunch U.S. support of Israel. Particular concerns include Israel's treatment of the Palestinians and its nuclear program, both of which lead to allegations that the United States has a double standard. Many Gulf citizens are also concerned about the suffering of the Iraqi people, for which sanctions are widely blamed. Outside of Kuwait, enforcement of the no-fly zones is often viewed as gratuitous cruelty: many Gulf residents believe the United States looks for pretexts to bomb Iraq and kill Muslims when possible. More generally, the United States is seen as a hegemonic power that seeks to spread its values and dominate the politics of weaker states. Conspiracy theories concerning the United States, and particularly the "true" purpose of its military forces, also abound.[25]

Area regimes have managed the tensions raised by the U.S. presence and security relationship successfully for the last decade (and, in several cases, for far longer) without facing massive instability. Moreover, although U.S. policy may be unpopular, it is of far less concern to most Gulf citizens than more basic issues such as government accountability and the overall economic performance. That said, an unpopular U.S. presence and policy can lead to increased pressure on the Gulf states and may act as a lightning rod for criticism.

DRAMATIC REGIME CHANGE IN IRAQ OR IRAN

Any discussion of unrest within U.S. partners should recognize that both Iran and Iraq face the possibility, although hardly the likelihood, of internally generated regime change in the coming years. U.S. adversary regimes are far less stable than those of U.S. partners, raising the prospect of an improvement, or at least a change, in the region's security environment.

---

[25]Byman and Green, *Political Violence and Stability in the States of the Northern Persian Gulf.*

In Iraq, most plausible successor regimes are likely to be friendlier toward the United States and its partners.[26] That said, the future Iraqi regime is difficult to predict. As Gary Sick notes, "Iraq is a brittle regime, heavily dependent on one man, and change could occur suddenly and unpredictably."[27] To prevent a challenge to his rule, Saddam has systematically crippled all other Iraqi institutions and civil society.[28] Should he die suddenly, it would be difficult for any successor to consolidate power. Moreover, given the individual nature of his regime, even a successor from the same power base that produced Saddam might pursue a vastly different foreign policy.

Instability in Iraq, however, poses an immediate threat to its neighbors in the form of refugees. Unrest and violence in Iraq, whether due to the collapse of the regime or a renewal of ethnic and sectarian pogroms by the Baath, could lead to refugee flows numbering in the hundreds of thousands. Many Kurds might flee and quickly overwhelm facilities in Turkey and Iran, while Shi'a might go to Kuwait and Saudi Arabia as well as to Iran. The humanitarian implications are considerable and the demographic balance in countries with small populations like Kuwait and Saudi Arabia could change overnight.

A regime not led by Saddam Husayn is likely to be less aggressive and less prone to miscalculation even if its leadership shares his expansionistic ambitions. Moreover, Iraq is not inherently an aggressor state. Although Iraq's near-landlocked status has led various regimes to seek a sea outlet through the Shatt al-Arab or through Kuwait, Iraq

---

[26]See Daniel Byman, "Iraq After Saddam," *The Washington Quarterly*, Autumn 2001, pp. 151–162, for a review. After the end of the Gulf War in 1991, U.S. officials feared that a collapse of the Baath regime in Iraq could lead to widespread instability and might allow Iran an opportunity to increase its influence in the region. Many officials also believed that U.S. partners in the region feared instability and would oppose U.S. policy if it might further destabilize Iraq. For a critique, see Byman, "Let Iraq Collapse," *The National Interest*, No. 45, Fall 1996, pp. 48–60, where he argues that the fear of Iranian influence is exaggerated and that instability in Iraq would reduce threats to U.S. partners.

[27]Gary Sick, "The Future of Iraq," *Middle East Policy*, Vol. 7, No. 4, October 2000, p. 60.

[28]See Regis W. Matlak, "Inside Saddam's Grip," *National Security Studies Quarterly*, Spring 1999, accessed from http://www.georgetown.edu/sfs/programs/nssp/nssq/Matlak.pdf, for a review.

could easily pursue the same goal through diplomacy and commercial incentives.[29]

Change is likely in Iran, although any shift is likely to be evolutionary and narrower in scope. The political system designed for the singular abilities of Ayatollah Khomeini has proven unfit for his successors. No actor or faction has proven able to consolidate power. As a result, reformers of all stripes and an array of conservatives are wrestling over fundamental issues such as the role of government in the economy, the proper level of free speech, the degree of state enforcement of social mores, and Iran's foreign policy orientation. Iran's unique political system, the *velayat-e faqih* (or rule of jurisprudence), is being increasingly questioned, both by secular Iranians and, more and more, by Iran's religious establishment, which views it as an incorrect interpretation of Islam that is corrupting religion in general.

The demographic problems that pose a challenge to the long-term stability of U.S. partners in the Persian Gulf, ironically, may prove favorable to U.S. interests in Iran. Although the clerical regime has successfully reduced the rate of population growth in recent years,[30] for over ten years after the revolution Iran's population grew more than 3 percent per year, leading to a bulge in the population cohort that is just entering the workforce. This demographic pressure augurs well for U.S. interests, because younger Iranians have been in the forefront of reform efforts and are less supportive of the clerical regime than is the older generation.

Thus, it is possible that an Iranian regime may emerge that is far less ideological, more open to the West, and more focused on Iran's economic needs. Such a regime would still have difficulties with the United States, particularly on the issue of WMD, which any Iranian regime would probably pursue. Nevertheless, a more moderate Iran would be far less threatening to the Gulf states and to U.S. interests overall.

---

[29]Al-Khafaji, "The Myth of Iraqi Exceptionalism," pp. 63–64.

[30]In 2000, for example, the population growth rate was less than 1 percent. See http://www.odci.gov/cia/publications/factbook/index.html.

Chapter Four

CONCLUSIONS

The likely challenges in the Gulf in the coming decade defy easy description. Many of the trends are positive, but several daunting problems remain that will pose challenges for the U.S. military and for U.S. policy. This final chapter reviews the implications of the above trends, suggesting areas that deserve greater attention in the coming years. The United States should focus less on the conventional military threat and more on the risk of WMD. Equally important, Washington must recognize the risk of instability in several Gulf partners, particularly in Saudi Arabia, and try to minimize any deleterious effects of the U.S. military presence.

THE SHIFTING CHALLENGE

Many of the threats that the United States and its partners have prepared for during the last decade have diminished. Iran's, and especially Iraq's, militaries have declined relative to those of the Gulf states, and their ability to conduct large-scale, sustained operations is highly questionable. Tehran's ability to subvert Gulf governments has also declined. Iraq's size and favorable terrain enable it to pose a continuing threat to Kuwait and Saudi Arabia, but this threat has declined over the past decade in the face of Gulf state military improvements, extensive U.S. forward presence and prepositioning, and improvements in U.S. rapid deployment capabilities. Because Iraq remains hostile and Iran's regime is in flux, the United States should tread cautiously. Nevertheless, U.S. planners should recognize that the traditional threats have decreased.[1]

Weapons of mass destruction remain a grave concern. The Iraqi program appears to have stalled, or is making only limited progress, as a result of a combination of sanctions, inspections, and international scrutiny. Iran's program also has not proceeded as quickly as expected for budget reasons and the declining Iraqi threat. That said, both Iran and Iraq seek all forms of WMD. Iraq has demonstrated that it will use WMD, and its willingness to suffer ten years of sanctions suggests its commitment to keeping its WMD programs. If sanctions are lifted, Baghdad is likely to make an aggressive effort to restore its WMD programs, and Tehran is likely to increase the pace of its effort in response.

Given conventional U.S. superiority, it is not likely that Iran or Iraq would challenge the United States directly without considering the use of WMD. Neither regime would openly threaten WMD lightly: such a threat is likely to occur only if the United States challenges the regime's very existence or the country's territorial integrity. The WMD threat may also be implicit—simply possessing ballistic missiles or other means of delivery with chemical, biological, or nuclear warheads may make the United States and its partners tread carefully.

THE CONFLICTING SECURITY DYNAMICS OF THE OIL MARKET

Oil prices per barrel over the next decade are predicted to be (in 1998 dollars) between $14.90 and $26.31, with the expected price at approximately $21.00 per barrel.[2] However, the track record of experts predicting oil prices is poor. During the 1970s, the U.S. Department of Energy anticipated that oil would reach $250 per barrel by the year 2000. Similarly, few in early 1999 anticipated that oil prices would

---

[1]Indeed, the United States must prepare for the possibility of widespread instability in Iran or Iraq. Although the U.S. partners in the Gulf face their own set of problems, they are not suffering the fundamental systemic crisis as is Iran today nor is their governing structure as brittle or individual dependent as that in Iraq. The possibility of civil war or widespread unrest in Iraq or Iran, while low, remains real.

[2]Energy Information Administration, *International Energy Outlook 2000*.

more than triple in the coming year, even temporarily.[3] Even in 2000, the marketplace misjudged how high oil prices would go.[4] Thus, the $14.90–$26.31 estimated range given above must be viewed with caution.

Whether oil prices are low or high, the Gulf will remain vital to the overall world supply. If oil prices are low, Gulf producers are likely to assume a greater percentage of overall production. Gulf production costs are among the lowest in the world, allowing Gulf producers to profit even if the price of oil plummets. Producers in the Caspian or North Sea, in contrast, can make a profit only when oil prices are high.[5] Should oil prices remain high, however, the importance of the Gulf states, along with all other producers, will grow because there will no longer be many producers waiting to increase production in response to a sudden supply disruption.

The security dynamics of the oil market are often contradictory. On the one hand, a higher oil price will enable Iran and Iraq to purchase more weapons and otherwise sustain their regimes. On the other hand, a low oil price will hurt U.S. partners as well as adversaries, increasing the risk of political instability in the region.

Low prices could have the following implications:

- Tension among states in the region.[6] Because Iran, unlike Iraq and Saudi Arabia, cannot increase production if the price of oil

---

[3]"Energy Survey," *The Economist*, February 10, 2001, p. 13. The Energy Department's prediction was in anticipated year 2000 prices.

[4]Saudi American Bank, "The Saudi Economy," p. 4.

[5]In Saudi Arabia, for example, production costs are approximately $1.50 per barrel, compared with more than ten times that price in the North Sea. Energy Information Administration, *International Energy Outlook 2000*. A long-term disruption is much less likely because of broad structural changes in the oil market. Lowered cost of operations, deeper drilling, and improved abilities to detect oil have greatly increased overall world oil reserves. Placke, "Low Oil Prices."

[6]Use of oil pricing and production to influence regional states is a common practice. In 1997, Saudi Arabia pushed the Organization of the Petroleum Exporting Countries (OPEC) to increase production in part to punish Iran for cheating on its oil quota. Richard, "New Cohesion in OPEC's Cartel?" After the May 1997 election of Mohammed Khatami in Iran, Saudi Arabia and Iran worked together to coordinate their policies within OPEC.

falls, it will suffer far more from a market collapse.[7] If Iraq or Saudi Arabia is viewed as causing this collapse through deliberate overproduction, it would generate tremendous anger in Tehran.

- Internal unrest in regional states. Almost all regional states' economies depend on oil. A low price of oil would decrease regimes' ability to buy off popular dissent but is not likely to significantly lower popular expectations of the government. Regimes may be forced to privatize state assets, reduce the size of the safety net, limit subsidies to businesses, cut largesse to ruling family members, and otherwise take politically difficult steps.

- Hinder Iran and Iraq's efforts to rebuild their militaries. As noted above, both Iran and Iraq need qualitative and quantitative improvements in their military forces if they are to regain past levels of effectiveness. These improvements will require a great deal of money, both for purchases and to maintain large numbers of men at arms. In Iran's case, budget constraints prevented it from making major arms purchases over the past decade and probably hindered its overall drive to develop nuclear weapons. Had Iraq not been restricted by sanctions, the low price of oil throughout most of the 1990s would have limited its purchases.[8]

High oil prices, of course, would have the opposite implications. Area regimes will simply have more—more to spend on government services, more to pass on to bolster local economies, and more to buy off dissent should it arise. The U.S. Embassy in Riyadh estimates that every $1 increase in the price of a barrel of oil provides the Saudi

---

[7]Iran does not have the excess capacity that Saudi Arabia and Iraq enjoy and its costs of extraction are higher. Bijan Zanganeh, Iran's petroleum minister, has claimed that enhanced recovery techniques greatly increase the recoverable amount of Iran's reserves. If true, this would increase Iran's ability to produce more and to sustain surge production. See Moin Siddiqi, "The Key to Iran's Prosperity," *The Middle East*, No. 307, December 2000, p. 34.

[8]U.S. partners, of course, will also spend less on defense. When oil prices fell in 1998, Saudi Arabia cut defense spending 22 percent. Steve Liesman, "Low Oil Prices Pressure Saudi Economy," *Wall Street Journal*, March 1, 1999, available at http://www.idrel.com.lb/shufme/archives/docsme/wsj990301.htm (downloaded May 21, 2001).

government with an additional $2.9 billion in annual revenues.[9] If the Gulf states choose to restructure their economies—a sensible long-term decision, but one that they avoided in the past when oil prices were high—they will be able to cushion many of the negative effects, such as higher initial unemployment. However, high prices will enable Iran and Iraq to rebuild their militaries more quickly and to acquire larger numbers of more sophisticated equipment.

LOOKING OUTSIDE THE MIDDLE EAST

Many of the potential problems in the Gulf that may arise in the coming decade have their solutions outside the region, and indeed outside the Middle East itself. Some key factors, such as the price of oil, are determined by international markets and are difficult for the United States to control. Others, such as the status of the Arab-Israeli conflict, are subject to U.S. influence but nevertheless remain difficult to manage, or even to predict.

The quality of the conventional weapons that Iran and Iraq will possess will be in large part determined by Russia and Europe, and China to a lesser degree. Whether Iran and Iraq possess advanced SAMs and antiship cruise missiles, are trained to use various sophisticated systems, and otherwise are able to acquire the capabilities needed to challenge the United States effectively depends more on decisions in Moscow or Paris than those in Baghdad or Tehran. During the 1990s, the United States effectively limited the flow of advanced weapons to Iran and to Iraq, but changes in U.S.-Europe or U.S.-Russia relationships could lead to greater problems in the Gulf.

The cooperation of outside powers is particularly important to halt WMD programs in Iran and Iraq. If Iran or Iraq could divert fissionable material, they could accelerate the time frame of their nuclear programs, perhaps acquiring a functional weapon within two years. Assistance in training technicians, developing civilian nuclear power, improving the accuracy of ballistic missile systems, or mastering other difficult tasks also would have a tremendous impact on the timetable and lethality of Iranian or Iraqi programs.

---

[9]United States Embassy in Riyadh, "Saudi Arabia: 2000 Economic Trends."

ANTICIPATING INSTABILITY WITHIN U.S. ADVERSARIES

The United States must prepare for the prospect of chronic and widespread instability in Iran or Iraq. Unrest in Iraq after the Gulf War led hundreds of thousands of Kurds and Shi'a to flee the country to Turkey and Iran and eventually led to the creation of protected zones in northern and southern Iraq. Another spate of unrest in Iraq could involve even more difficult problems. Warring factions might use WMD against each other or against civilians seen as supporting their rivals. Iran and Turkey might intervene directly to eradicate domestic opposition groups currently based in Iraq. If unrest occurred in Iran, Iraq might try to readjust the long-disputed border over the Shatt al-Arab. Both countries' neighbors would seize on any instability to put their proxies in power, or at least to undermine those of their rivals.

Even if the regimes do not collapse, it is possible that leaders in these countries might try to divert domestic instability by creating a crisis abroad. Iranian conservatives have already tried to rally support by criticizing the United States—growing domestic unrest might lead them to become even more confrontational. Saddam in the past has used adventurism abroad to bolster his support at home and increased strife might lead him to become more aggressive.

Instability in either country might multiply the tasks required of the U.S. military. If regimes use foreign adventures to divert domestic discontent, U.S. attempts to deter aggression will be far more difficult. If governments collapse, U.S. forces might be called on to assist in humanitarian relief, to secure WMD, to prevent outside meddling, or even to aid a preferred faction in coming to power.

PREPARING FOR ANTI-U.S. PRESSURE AMONG PARTNERS

The United States currently has achieved a balance between its military requirements in the Gulf and the ability of regional partners to host and work with U.S. forces. Although the size and positioning of U.S. forces may shift in response to various political or economic requirements of U.S. partners, in general the U.S. mix of low visibility, reliance on multiple states for prepositioning and forward presence, and increased military engagement has satisfied Gulf states without jeopardizing their stability.

Nevertheless, as discussed in Chapter Three, the Gulf states may face pressure to decrease ties to the United States, particularly to the U.S. military. The U.S. presence may grow unpopular in conjunction with other U.S. policies that are viewed with disfavor in the region (particularly with regard to the Arab-Israeli conflict), U.S. support for Gulf regimes that are increasingly at odds with their populations, social crises that lead to criticism of Westernizing influences, or other, unanticipated, problems. The U.S. military presence may act as a lightning rod for criticism. In addition, governments facing restive populations may be loathe to further provoke them by making unpopular foreign policy decisions that involve cooperating with the United States.

Such problems are not likely to lead to a complete rupture with the United States, but they may make the operating environment difficult for the United States in a variety of ways. Possible problems include:

- Placing limits on U.S. operations. Over the last ten years, Gulf regimes have regularly placed limits on the use of force against Iraq.[10] Increased popular input into decisionmaking may make the regimes more likely to avoid supporting operations that are seen as victimizing Iraq or the Iraqi people. This may include refusing a U.S. request to enforce the so-called "no-drive zone," which is important for the defense of Kuwait.

- Responding slowly during a crisis. Even if Gulf regimes permit the United States to overfly their territory and have access to bases on their soil for operations, they may not respond to these requests quickly, leading to costly delays.

- Limiting support for other U.S. initiatives in the region. Gulf regimes may find it difficult to support U.S. positions on the Arab-Israeli conflicts, on proliferation in the region, and on other contentious issues.

- Reducing military purchases in general, including from U.S. arms companies.

---

[10]For a review, see Byman and Waxman, *Confronting Iraq.*

- Reducing the overall size, or at least the visibility, of the U.S. military presence. Such pressure is particularly likely in Saudi Arabia, where interviews suggest that popular opinion appears to be strongly against the U.S. military presence. One observer summarized the Saudi point of view toward the U.S. presence as: "We want you to be like the wind. We want to feel you, but we don't want to see you."[11]

FINAL WORDS

The above problems are not insurmountable for the United States. Indeed, in many respects they are easier to meet than the more traditional problems or Iranian or Iraqi aggression. Meeting these challenges, however, requires several shifts for USAF and U.S. military planners. Most important, they require anticipating a range of less traditional concerns, such as the threat of WMD and the potential for domestic unrest among U.S. partners. In addition, they require recognizing that the U.S. position in the Gulf depends heavily on events outside the region. Finally, planners must recognize that partners may be less willing to cooperate openly with Washington in the future. Recognizing these shifts will enable the United States to secure its interests in the Gulf region in the coming decade.

---

[11]As quoted in Alterman, "The Gulf States and the American Umbrella."

MILITARY STRENGTH IN THE GULF STATES

Table A.1

Gross Measures of Military Strength in the Gulf

Country	Army	MBT	Quality MBT	All GCV	Total Artillery Attack	Helicopters	Combat Aircraft	Modern Combat Aircraft	Surface Combatants
Iran	325,000	1,495	715	2,640	2,794	100	236	212	28
Iraq	375,000	2,200	1,000	6,600	2,100	120	210	112	1
Bahrain	8,500	106	106	517	107	40	24	24	11
Kuwait	11,000	385	293	748	86	16	54	54	10
Oman	25,000	117	117	378	120	0	24	0	13
Qatar	8,500	44	44	328	44	19	18	12	7
UAE	59,000	331	331	1,509	312	47	65	65	18
Saudi Arabia	75,000	1,055	710	3,900	450	24	343	343	34
Saudi/Kuwait	86,000	1,440	1,003	4,648	536	40	397	397	44
Saudi/GCC	187,000	2,038	1,601	7,380	1,119	146	528	498	93

Table A.2
Combat Units in the Gulf

Country	HQ Unit	Army Combat Unit			Special "Guard" Unit	Combat Air Squadron
		Division	Brigade	Battalion		
Iran	4 corps	4 armored division 6 infantry division	1 airborne brigade		16–20 division (2 armd, 5 mech, 10 infantry, 1 Special Forces, and 15–20 indep brigade)	5 FGA 7 FTR
Iraq	7 corps	3 armored division 3 mechanized division 12 infantry division			6 division (2 armored, 3 mechanized, 1 infantry) 4 Special Republican Guard brigade	17 FTR/FGA
Bahrain			1 armored brigade 1 infantry brigade 1 artillery brigade	1 Special Forces battalion 1 air defense battalion		1 FGA 1 FTR

Table A.2—continued

Country	HQ Unit	Division	Brigade	Battalion	Special "Guard" Unit	Combat Air Squadron
			Army Combat Unit			
Kuwait			2 armored brigade 1 artillery brigade 1 mechanized infantry brigade 1 engineering brigade 1 reconnaissance (mechanized) brigade 1 armored brigade 2 infantry brigade HQ 2 armored regiment 1 armored reconnaissance regiment			4 FTR/FGA
Oman			4 artillery regiment 1 armored division regiment 8 infantry regiment 1 airborne regiment 1 engineering regiment			

Table A.2—continued

			Army Combat Unit			
Country	HQ Unit	Division	Brigade	Battalion	Special "Guard" Unit	Combat Air Squadron
Qatar				1 Special Forces battalion 1 armored battalion 4 mechanized infantry battalion 1 mortar battalion	1 Guard regiment	2 FTR/FGA
UAE			1 armored brigade 2 mechanized infantry brigade 2 infantry brigade		1 Guard brigade	3 FTR 1 FGA
Saudi Arabia			3 armored brigade 5 mechanized brigade 1 airborne brigade	8 artillery battalion 1 army aviation command	1 Guard regiment	11 FTR 7 FGA

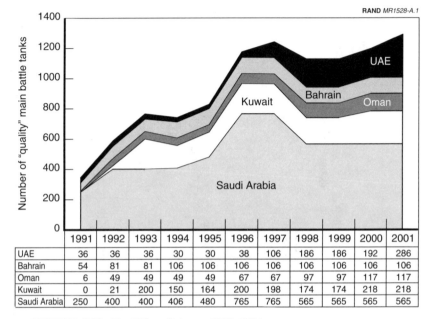

SOURCE: IISS, *The Military Balance, 2000–2001.*

Figure A.1—Gulf States' "Quality" Main Battle Tanks

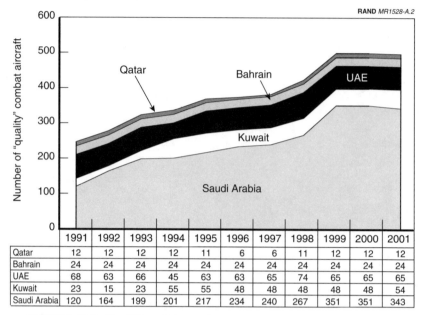

	1991	1992	1993	1994	1995	1996	1997	1998	1999	2000	2001
Qatar	12	12	12	12	11	6	6	11	12	12	12
Bahrain	24	24	24	24	24	24	24	24	24	24	24
UAE	68	63	66	45	63	63	65	74	65	65	65
Kuwait	23	15	23	55	55	48	48	48	48	48	54
Saudi Arabia	120	164	199	201	217	234	240	267	351	351	343

SOURCE: IISS, *The Military Balance, 2000–2001.*

Figure A.2—Gulf States ' "Quality" Combat Aircraft

BIBLIOGRAPHY

Al-Khafaji, Isam, "The Myth of Iraqi Exceptionalism," *Middle East Policy*, Vol. 7, No. 4, October 2000, pp. 62–86.

Alnajjar, Ghanim, "The GCC and Iraq," *Middle East Policy*, Vol. 7, No. 4, October 2000, pp. 92–99.

Alterman, Jon, "The Gulf States and the American Umbrella," *Middle East Review of International Affairs*, Vol. 4, No. 4, December 2000, electronic version.

Amirahmadi, H., "Economic Costs of the War and Reconstruction in Iran," in C. Bina and H. Zangeneh (eds.), *Modern Capitalism and Islamic Ideology in Iran*, St. Martin's Press, New York, 1992.

Axelgard, Fred, "Iraq and the War with Iran," *Current History*, February 1987, pp. 57–82.

"Bahrain: Defendants' Confessions Reported," Manama WAKH, FBIS-NES-96-110, June 5, 1996.

"Bahrain: Interior Ministry on Arrest of 'Hizballah of Bahrain' Group," Manama WAKH, FBIS-NES-96-107, June 3, 1996.

Baram, Amatzia, *Building Toward Crises: Saddam Hussein's Strategy for Survival*, Washington Institute for Near East Policy, Washington, D.C., 1998.

Barkey, Henri J., "Hemmed in by Circumstances: Turkey and Iraq Since the Gulf War," *Middle East Policy*, Vol. 7, No. 4, October 2000, pp. 110–126.

Bensahel, Nora, "Political Reform in the Middle East," in Nora Bensahel and Daniel Byman (eds.), *Security Trends in the Middle East and Their Implications for the United States*, RAND, forthcoming.

Borger, Julian, "Iraq Rearming for War, Say Defectors," *The Guardian*, April 29, 2002.

Boyne, Sean, and Salameh Nematt, "Baghdad Resurgent," *Jane's Defence Weekly*, July 25, 2001.

"BP Amoco Statistical Review of World Energy 2000," available at http://www.bpamaco.com/worldenergy (accessed March 5, 2001).

Brooks, Risa, "Civil-Military Relations in the Middle East," in Nora Bensahel and Daniel Byman (eds.), *Security Trends in the Middle East and Their Implications for the United States*, RAND, forthcoming.

Burns, Robert, "U.S. Beefs Up Airbase in Qatar," *Associated Press*, July 2, 2002.

Byman, Daniel, "Iraq After Saddam," *The Washington Quarterly*, Autumn 2001, pp. 151–162.

_____, "Let Iraq Collapse," *The National Interest*, No. 45, Fall 1996, pp. 48–60.

_____, Shahram Chubin, Anoushiravan Ehteshami, and Jerrold Green, *Iran's Security Policy in the Post-Revolutionary Era*, RAND, MR-1320-OSD, 2001.

_____, and Roger Cliff, *China's Arms Sales: Motivations and Implications*, RAND, MR-1119-AF, 1999.

_____, and Jerrold Green, *Political Violence and Stability in the States of the Northern Persian Gulf*, RAND, MR-1021-OSD, 1999.

_____, and Matthew Waxman, *Confronting Iraq: U.S. Policy and the Use of Force Since the Gulf War*, RAND, MR-1146-OSD, 2000.

"Can Crown Prince Abdullah Lead His Desert Kingdom into the 21st Century?" *Business Week*, May 21, 2001, available at http://www.

businessweek.com:/2000/00_30/b3691008.htm (accessed May 19, 2001).

Cockburn, Andrew, and Patrick Cockburn, *Out of the Ashes: The Resurrection of Saddam Hussein,* HarperCollins, New York, 1999.

Cohen, Eliot (ed.), *Gulf War Air Power Survey,* Vol. 2, Office of the Secretary of the Air Force, Washington, D.C., 1993.

Cordesman, Anthony H., *The Military Balance in the Gulf, Vol. III: Southern Gulf Forces,* Center for Strategic and International Studies, Washington, D.C., 1998.

_____, *Bahrain, Oman, Qatar, and the UAE: Challenges of Security,* Westview Press, Boulder, CO, 1997.

_____, *If We Fight Iraq: Iraq and the Conventional Military Balance,* Center for Strategic and International Studies, Washington, D.C., January 31, 2002.

_____, *Iran's Military Forces in Transition: Conventional Threats and Weapons,* Praeger, Westport, CT, 1999.

_____, *The Military Balance in the Gulf, Vol. IV: The Southern Gulf,* Center for Strategic and International Studies, Washington, D.C., 1998.

_____, "The Persian-Arabian Gulf and the Revolution in Military Affairs," *National Security Studies Quarterly,* Vol. 6, No. 32, Summer 2000, pp. 81–89.

_____, and Ahmed Hashim, *Iraq: Sanctions and Beyond,* Westview Press, Boulder, CO, 1997.

David, Steven R., "Saving America from the Coming Civil Wars," *Foreign Affairs,* Vol. 78, No. 1, January/February 1999, pp. 103–116.

Einhorn, Robert J., testimony before the Senate Foreign Relations Committee, October 5, 2000.

Eisenstadt, Michael, "The Armed Forces of the Islamic Republic of Iran: An Assessment," *Middle East Review of International Affairs,* Vol. 5, No. 1, December 2000, electronic version.

_____, *Iranian Military Power: Capabilities and Intentions*, Washington Institute for Near East Policy, Washington, D.C., 1996.

_____, *Iraq's Weapons of Mass Destruction (WMD): An Emerging Challenge for the Bush Administration*, Washington Institute for Near East Policy, Washington, D.C., January 26, 2001.

_____, "Recent Changes in Saddam's Inner Circle: Cracks in the Wall?" *Policywatch* 22, November 22, 1991.

El Eslam Hasan Rowhani, Hojjat, Vice-Speaker of the Majles [parliament], Islamic Republic News Agency, BBC ME/ 3700MED/7, November 24, 1999.

Energy Information Administration, *Annual Energy Outlook 2001*, available at http://www.eia.doe.gov/oiaf/aeo/economic.html# international (accessed March 13, 2001).

Energy Information Administration, *International Energy Outlook 2000*, March 31, 2000, available at http://www.eia.doe.gov/oiaf/ ieo.html (accessed January 17, 2001).

Energy Information Administration, "Iran" (September 2000), available at http://www.eia.doe.gov/emeu/cabs/iran.html (accessed January 16, 2001).

Energy Information Administration, "Iraq" (September 2000), available at http://www.eia.doe.gov/emeu/cabs/iraq.html (accessed January 16, 2001).

Energy Information Administration, "OPEC Revenues: Country Details" (October 2000), available at http://www.eia.doe.gov/ emeu/cabs/orevcoun.html (accessed January 16, 2001).

Energy Information Administration, "OPEC Revenues Fact Sheet" (October 2000), available at http://www.eia.doe.gov/emeu.cabs. opecrev2.html (accessed January 16, 2001).

Energy Information Administration, "Saudi Arabia" (November 2000), available at http://www.eia.doe.gov/cabs/saudi2.html (accessed January 16, 2001).

"Energy Survey," *The Economist*, February 10, 2001, pp. 1–24 (survey section).

Fried, Edward R., and Philip H. Trezise, *Oil Security: Retrospect and Prospect*, Brookings Institution, Washington, D.C., 1993.

Fuller, Graham, and Rend Rahim Francke, *The Arab Shi'a: The Forgotten Muslims*, St. Martin's Press, New York, 1999.

Gause, F. Gregory III, *Oil Monarchies: Domestic and Security Challenges in the Arab Gulf States*, Council on Foreign Relations Press, New York, 1993.

_____, "Saudi Arabia Over a Barrel," *Foreign Affairs*, Vol. 79, No. 3, May/June 2000, pp. 80–94.

Graham, Bradley, and Thomas Ricks, "Contingency Plan Shifts Saudi Base to Qatar; US Wants to Lessen Dependence on Riyadh," *Washington Post*, April 6, 2002.

Henderson, Simon, "Arab Gulf Politics and Powell's Visit," *Policywatch* 520, Washington Institute for Near East Policy, Washington, D.C., February 26, 2001.

_____, *The Gulf Cooperation Council Defense Pact: An Exercise in Ambiguity*, Washington Institute for Near East Policy, Washington, D.C., January 16, 2001, electronic version.

International Institute of Strategic Studies, *The Military Balance, 1999–2000*, London, 2000.

_____, *The Military Balance, 2000–2001*, London, 2001.

"The Iranian Arms Effort," *Gulf States Newsletter*, Vol. 25, No. 634, April 17, 2000, pp. 8–10.

Jane's Sentinel Security Assessment, *Iraq—Air Force*, January 9, 2002.

Jane's Sentinel Security Assessment, *Saudi Arabia—Armed Forces*, July 3, 2002.

Kanovsky, Eliyahu, *Iran's Economic Morass: Mismanagement and Decline Under the Islamic Republic*, WINEP, 1997.

Kechichian, Joseph A., *Oman and the World: The Emergence of an Independent Foreign Policy*, RAND, MR-680-RC, 1995.

"Khatami Has Bumpy Trip in Russia," Radio Free Europe/Radio Liberty Iran Report, Vol. 4, No. 11, March 19, 2001, electronic version.

Kostiner, Joseph, "Low Oil Prices: Implications for the Gulf Monarchies," talk at the Washington Institute for Near East Policy, Washington, D.C., July 15, 1998.

Kreisel, W., "Health Situation in Iraq," testimony presented at the European Union Committee on Foreign Affairs, Human Rights, Common Security, and Defense Policy, Brussels, Belgium, February 26, 2001, electronic version.

Lambeth, Benjamin S., *The Transformation of American Air Power*, Cornell University Press, Ithaca, NY, 2000.

Liesman, Steve, "Low Oil Prices Pressure Saudi Economy," *Wall Street Journal*, March 1, 1999, available at http://www.idrel.com.lb/shufme/archives/docsme/wsj990301.htm (downloaded May 21, 2001).

Lynch, Colum, "UN Council Approves Revision of Iraqi Sanctions," *Washington Post*, May 14, 2002.

Marr, Phebe, "Comments," *Middle East Policy*, Vol. 7, No. 4, October 2000, pp. 87–91.

_____, *The Modern History of Iraq*, Westview Press, Boulder, CO, 1985, pp. 180–181.

Martin, Lenore, *The Unstable Gulf: Threats from Within*, Lexington Books, Lexington, MA, 1984.

Matlak, Regis W., "Inside Saddam's Grip," *National Security Studies Quarterly*, Spring 1999, accessed from http://www.georgetown.edu/sfs/programs/nssp/nssq/Matlak.pdf.

Palmer, Michael A., *Guardians of the Gulf: A History of America's Expanding Role in the Persian Gulf, 1833–1992*, The Free Press, New York, 1992.

Parasiliti, Andrew, and Sinan Antoon, "Friends in Need, Foes to Heed: The Iraqi Military in Politics," *Middle East Policy*, Vol. 7, No. 4, October 2000, pp. 134–138.

Partrick, Neil, "Weapons of Mass Destruction and the Threat to the Gulf," speech given to the Royal United Services Institute Gulf Security Conference 2000 in London, June 2000.

Pisik, Betsy, "Iraqi Trade Doing Fine Despite Sanctions," *Washington Times*, October 25, 2000, p. 1.

Placke, James, "Low Oil Prices: Implications for the Gulf Monarchies," talk at the Washington Institute for Near East Policy, Washington, D.C., July 15, 1998.

Pollack, Kenneth, "The Influence of Arab Culture on Arab Military Effectiveness," unpublished dissertation, Cambridge, MA, 1996.

Powell, Colin L., "Opening Statement Before the Senate Foreign Relations Committee," March 8, 2001.

Prados, Alfred B., "Saudi Arabia: Post-War Issues and U.S. Relations," *CRS Issue Brief*, December 2, 1996, http://www.fas.org/man/crs/3-113.htm (accessed March 8, 2001).

Quandt, William, "The Middle East on the Brink: Prospects for Change," *Middle East Journal*, Vol. 50, No. 1, Winter 1996.

_____, *Saudi Arabia in the 1980s: Foreign Policy, Security, and Oil*, The Brookings Institution, Washington, D.C., 1981.

Ramazani, R. K., *Revolutionary Iran*, Johns Hopkins Press, Baltimore, MD, 1988.

Richard, James, "New Cohesion in OPEC's Cartel? Pricing and Politics," *Middle East Review of International Affairs*, Vol. 3, No. 2, June 1999, electronic version.

Richards, Alan, "The Political Economy of Economic Reform in the Middle East," in Nora Bensahel and Daniel Byman (eds.) *Security Trends in the Middle East and Their Implications for the United States*, RAND, forthcoming.

Richter, Paul, "Scientist Warns of Iraq's Nuclear Gains," *Los Angeles Times*, August 1, 2002.

Ritter, Scott, "The Case for Iraq's Qualitative Disarmament," *Arms Control Today*, June 2000, pp. 8–14.

Rumer, Eugene, *Dangerous Drift: Russia's Middle East Policy*, Washington Institute for Near East Policy, Washington, D.C., 2000.

Safran, Nadav, *Saudi Arabia: The Ceaseless Quest for Security*, Cornell University Press, Ithaca, NY, 1988.

Saudi American Bank, "The Saudi Economy: 2001 Performance, 2001 Forecast," available at www.samba.com.sa (downloaded May 23, 2001).

"The Saudi Economy Crisis: Entrance and Exit," available at http://www.miraserve.com/pressrev/eprev76.htm (downloaded May 23, 2001).

Schmitt, Eric, and Thom Shanker, "American Arsenal in the Mideast Is Being Built Up to Confront Saddam Hussein," *New York Times*, August 19, 2002.

Sciolino, Elaine, *Persian Mirrors: The Elusive Face of Iran*, The Free Press, New York, 2000.

Sick, Gary, "The Future of Iraq," *Middle East Policy*, Vol. 7, No. 4, October 2000, pp. 58–61.

Siddiqi, Moin, "The Key to Iran's Prosperity," *The Middle East*, No. 307, December 2000, pp. 34–37.

Slevin, Peter, and Glenn Kessler, "U.S. to Seek Mideast Reforms; Programs Aim to Foster Democracy, Education, Markets," *Washington Post*, August 21, 2002.

Smil, Vaclav, "The Energy Question, Again," *Current History*, Vol. 99, No. 641, December 1, 2000, pp. 408–412.

"Special Report on Saudi Arabia," *Middle East Economic Digest*, March 16, 2001, p. 30.

Stillion, John, and David T. Orletsky, *Airbase Vulnerability to Conventional Cruise-Missile and Ballistic-Missile Attacks: Technology, Scenarios, and U.S. Air Force Responses*, RAND, MR-1028-AF, 1999.

United States Embassy Riyadh, "Saudi Arabia: 2000 Economic Trends," April 2000, available at http://www.usembassy.state.gov/riyadh/wwwhet00.html (downloaded May 21, 2001).

United States Secretary of Defense, *Report on Allied Contributions to the Common Defense*, March 2000, pp. III-28 and D-10 through D-12.

Weaver, Mary Anne, "Democracy by Decree," *The New Yorker*, November 20, 2000, pp. 54–61.